THE ISRAEL OMEN

THE
ISRAEL
OMEN

The Ancient Warning
of Catastrophies Has Begun

DAVID BRENNAN

The Israel Omen

Website for book: www.IsraelOmen.com

Published by Teknon Publishing, Metairie, Louisiana.

ISBN Number: 978-0-578-03370-9

Retailers and distributors qualify for special discounts on bulk purchases. For more information, please contact Customer Service at Teknon Publishing 1-866-456-8988.

To my wonderful parents Ed and Alice Brennan;
61 years of marriage and counting!

With pleasure a special thanks is extended to all that helped with the editing and proofing process. To my old friend Clarke Kissel, also Marcia Wall and Susan Meindl for the professional job all did in editing. For their laborious effort in proofing I thank my parents, Ed and Alice Brennan, both of my sons, Paul and David as well as my old friend Charlie Abadie.

Important Recognition:
In their excellent book, ISRAEL THE BLESSING OR THE CURSE, John McTernan and William Koenig exhaustively catalogue numerous coincidences of disasters occurring during efforts to remove the "Promised Land" from the Jews. Their work was pioneering.

TABLE OF CONTENTS

PROLOGUE

The desert was viewed as impassable, a barren wasteland no army could endure, lest it be consumed by endless dunes. To Ottoman forces protecting the port city of Aqaba, the desert provided a natural barrier for that side of the city from attack. With the sea on the other side, it appeared impregnable. The notion of heavily fortifying the desert against attack seemed useless, even worse, a waste of resources desperately needed on other fronts of the Great War. But the sea, considered the only other approach to attack the city, was another matter. Since the sea represented the "only" option for an enemy to seize the port, Ottoman forces heavily fortified it, leaving the desert side almost undefended. Confident in their strategy of protecting the port from the growing Arab insurgency, led by British officer Thomas Lawrence, the Ottomans concluded that this small part of their vast Middle East Empire was safe. That would soon change. Lawrence, better known as Lawrence of Arabia for his military achievements on the Arabian Peninsula, would accomplish what many had viewed as the impossible. Leading his great army of Arab fighters through the desert, he struck the Ottoman forces at their weakest point, taking Aqaba and adding to his legend. Lawrence's many exploits during the war would rob the Ottomans of supplies and troops needed elsewhere, weakening them, and adding his own mark in the "war to end all wars."[1,2]

As rulers of the Middle East in 1914, when the First World War broke out, the Ottoman Empire made the mistake of siding with the Central powers in that European conflict, backing the German Kaiser in a gamble destined to fail.[3] This mistake would lead to the breakup of their great Middle East Empire in 1920, divided among the victors by the new League of Nations. The main recipients of this booty were France and Britain, both still thirsting for empires to govern. Within the British spoils came Palestine, made up of Jews and Arabs constituting the Palestinian population of the region. The British would rule Palestine during the 1920s and 1930s, and, then, through World War Two. However, not long after the end of that war, the British would conclude, like the Romans 2000 years earlier, that Palestine was ungovernable; consisting of "unreasonable" people.[4] As a result, they would turn it over to the newly formed United Nations to dispose of in a manner the members saw fitting. The U.N. would decide to divide it between the Arabs and Jews living within the area.[5]

After deliberations and agreement, especially between the United States and the Soviet Union, the new borders for Palestine were drawn with care, creating a map according to the density of Jewish and Arab populations. In 1947 the "United Nations Special Commission on Palestine" recommended dividing the area into an Arab state and a Jewish state. On November 29, 1947, the UN General Assembly, under resolution GA 181, approved the division and disposition of the lands accordingly.[6]

With resolution GA 181, the world had just approved a homeland for the Jews, their first in over 2000 years. But unbeknownst to its members on that chilly day in November, the United Nations had just fulfilled an ancient prophecy that foretold the eventual return of the Jews to the land of their ancestors. The new nation would be called Israel.[7]

CHAPTER ONE

Acts of God

It was one of the most moving scenes in the 20th Century-Fox thriller "The Omen" by David Seltzer. Jeremy Thorn, America's ambassador to the Court of Saint James, had grudgingly gone to meet the priest Tassone at Kew Gardens, a park in London. Tassone's intent was to warn the Ambassador of his son Damien's real identity, that of the anti-Christ Biblically foretold. Upon arriving to meet the priest, Thorn was met by these words:

> When the Jews return to Zion, and a comet rips the sky, and the Holy Roman Empire rises, then you and I must die. From the eternal sea he rises, creating armies on either shore, turning man against his brother. Til man exists no more![1]

The response of Thorn was not very favorable. But Tassone's opening line is an interesting one as it relates to another kind of omen, perhaps one that is actually unfolding within our midst today. Tassone's words are grounded in prophecy taken from the ancient Hebrew texts of the Old Testament and reaching all the way to the Book of Revelations. The phrase "when the Jews return to Zion" was placed first in the recital for a reason; the Jews had to return to the "Promised Land" before any of the other events could unfold.

And in 1948, after over 2000 years of being *scattered among the heathen,* (Old Testament) they did just that, causing a great stir among those that look for such signs. But does their return, in fact, represent a real omen for mankind, perhaps one he has been slow to recognize because belief in such things has waned over the centuries? In consideration of that question, there is this:

SINCE 1991...

* Hundreds of thousands have been displaced by the most destructive storms in U.S. history.

* The strongest earthquake ever recorded in an urban area in U.S. history hitting California.

* A once in a 500 year flood described as the "worst natural disaster in U.S. history" striking the Midwest.

* Over the course of a month, 562 tornadoes ripped through America's heartland in what was described as the "worst weather in U.S. history."

* A heat wave described as the worst in the past 250 years of European history plagued that continent.

* American soil was successfully attacked for the first time since Pearl Harbor with the attack on 9/11.

* A worldwide financial system meltdown, comparable only to the Great Depression, crippling nations around the world.

It should be noted that none of these catastrophes were minor as all were historical in their nature of destructiveness. Although all of these furious events would appear to be random acts of God, they strangely possessed one thing in common: timing that was uncannily associated with efforts to reverse a specific promise to the Jews, as recorded in ancient Hebrew texts. The promise in question pertains to the possession of lands located in the Middle East and referred to over time as the "Promised Land" of Israel.

This idea is, of course, a difficult one for many to accept. Some readers may immediately dismiss its legitimacy. In fact, such an implication was one this author had not considered when beginning the journey that eventually led to writing "The Israel Omen." However, in researching claims made by others, that destructive event's were taking place which coincided with efforts to remove part of the fabled "Promised Land," it became obvious that the coincidences were surprisingly real. The best source dealing with such coincidences is McTernan & Koenig's book. Of the ten "coincidences" reviewed here, the first nine were discovered in their book, ISRAEL THE BLESSING OR THE CURSE. Yet, the whole notion runs counter to beliefs that are well ingrained in the thoughts of contemporary man. But, as the reader will see, there is simply no denying that the timing of each of these events is strangely "coincidental" to efforts that challenge the ancient promise to the Jews given in those old writings.

There is more. There are additional ancient Hebrew writings that appear to be unfolding with an impressive degree of accuracy. These texts, also written some 2500 years ago, describe events that would take place sometime in the future and appear to line up so specifically with current circumstances in the Middle East conflict, as to have an eerie quality about them. The global financial meltdown that began in 2007 appears to fit all too well with a specific warning: efforts to remove the "Promised Land" would produce a global event that would "terrify" the nations. Again, although that statement may produce doubt for many, in chapters thirteen and fourteen the reader will see the case for such an outlandish claim.

Because the catastrophes reviewed all began in 1991, many readers will have a personal memory relating to them. In some of the cases discussed, such as 9/11, Hurricane Katrina and the global financial crisis, every reader should recall the event. For many, the catastrophe discussed will represent a personal experience of great difficulty. As one of those displaced by Katrina, eventually returning to a city of MREs (meals ready to eat) and M16s, this author understands that possibility well.

WHAT PROMISE TO THE JEWS?

Many people do not believe that the writings of the Biblical Old Testament reveal any promise by God to the Jews. But, in fact, they do. The Old Testament details specific promises to the Jews, which state that certain lands in the Middle East are an inheritance from God to them. (This promise and the description of these lands are handled in some detail in Appendix A in the back of the book, and will be referred to throughout). Included within these "Promised Lands" are the West Bank, Gaza, and the Golan Heights, all of which are at the center of much conflict and contention today.

In addition to naming the lands that were given to the Jews, these same ancient texts described what the future would hold for them, as it pertains to their nation. After possessing the land for a number of centuries, in 70 A.D., the Roman Empire,[3] which controlled that region as a vassal province, in an act of retribution against the rebellious Jews, destroyed the city of Jerusalem, scattering its people across the known world. This period of displacement is referred to in Jewish history as the great "Diaspora." Many were sold into slavery, and many more went wherever they would be accepted. Eventually, becoming a people spread across the world. The most impressive Hebrew texts are the ones that foretold the great "Diaspora," or scattering of the Jews, just as it would later unfold. Then, after the Jewish people were *scattered among the heathen,* they returned again in the distant future. This too was foretold. Today, one need only watch the nightly news to hear about the activities of Israel, a nation that did not exist for over 2000 years and now exists once again. This return to the "Promised Land," after for so long having been scattered across the globe, brought declarations that a significant Biblical prophecy had been fulfilled.

Now, another statement must be unleashed on the reader which will press the imagination further. It certainly did mine, until I did the math for myself. There is a mathematical prediction given all the way back in the 500s B.C. that appears to have foretold the very year the Jews would return to the land of their ancestors to form the reborn nation of Israel. That statement, as brazen as it is, is supported by the ancient Hebrew prophet Ezekiel as well, and is covered in detail within Appendix B. Essentially it looks at ancient Hebrew warnings to the Jews that describe what punishment would await them for their continued disobedience against God. Having continued in this disobedient state, they endure punishment that unfolds over a period of some 2500 years until the year 1948, the year the nation of Israel was reborn.

These prophetic utterances are significant in establishing a basis from which to consider the multitude of disasters that have taken place since 1991, relative to attempts to reverse the old promises. Since Israel came back into existence in the year 1948, it appears that land has become a danger for any nation attempting to alter the promises given to the Jews concerning it. If true, that is, indeed, a bad omen for mankind.

So, with this perspective in mind, it is time to consider the ancient words of a man that lived over 2500 years ago, and who foretold the history of the Jews for the last two thousand years.

CHAPTER TWO

The Man Who Saw the Future

Since the earliest of times mankind has been intrigued with the notion of seeing into the future, to know what terrible event might be racing toward a nation, or on a more personal level, toward an individual. Over the course of time many people have claimed to possess the ability to see into the future. The witch of En Dor, a woman of Biblical fame, was consulted by King Saul of the Israelites for insight into a coming battle.[1] The priestess of the oracle at Delphi claimed to hear prophetic utterances from the Greek god Apollo, after entering into a trance.[2] Of more recent notoriety is Nostradamus, whose written words purport to describe events yet to happen. After closer scrutiny, however, the claims of each appear to be dubious at best, possessing a very confusing and often cryptic nature. But there is another person from the distant past who is purported to have seen into the future, his words having stood up to the test of time.

Sometime in the 6th century B.C. a man named Ezekiel, whose words were recorded in the Book of the Old Testament of the same name, lived in the Middle East. Born in Jerusalem, he was reported to be among those brought into Babylonian captivity by King Nebuchadnezzar after Israel lost a war with Babylon. While in captivity, he describes a vision from God that he recorded in writings. The vision brought to him a revelation concerning the future of the small Middle Eastern nation of Israel. The vision indicated that the nation would be dissolved, its people *scattered among the heathens* of the world, only to be restored at a time in the distant future back to the very same lands it had previously possessed. The most famous of those predictions is titled *The Valley of Dry Bones*.[3]

THE VALLEY OF DRY BONES

The rebirth of Israel was as improbable an event as any in the history of mankind. How could a people, dispersed across the globe for 2000 years, gather themselves to become a nation again in the land their fore-fathers had long ago lived? It is difficult enough to imagine gathering a small group of people together from various parts of one nation for a family reunion, let alone a multitude coming together from many differ-ent countries for the creation of a nation. But as improbable as that was, it strangely took place in 1948, leaving many to wonder how such a thing could happen in this modern age. In fact, in a modern age where any trace of ancient tribes, dispersed long ago by war, are unable to be found except in the history books.

The rebirth of Israel was clearly foretold by Ezekiel in *The Valley of Dry Bones*. That passage describes a rebirth that was to take place after the Jewish people had been scattered throughout the world, with their com-ing back together again to be achieved under the most unlikely circum-stances. Ezekiel describes the events that took place in 1948 in writings that date back over 2500 years ago!

To get the gist of how unlikely their rebirth would be, try to imagine the following: A person just died on an operating table and is brought back to life. This we can imagine fairly easily as we hear about it occa-sionally in our modern day. Now let's take it a step further. A deceased person is being carried to their burial and is brought back to life. This would leave most of us in a state of awe. Now consider a significantly more extreme case than either of the first two. A deceased person has been buried for three days, is brought back to life and is now walking, talking, and eating among us. Such an event would defy the basis of life and death that is ingrained in our human experience and consciousness, and we simply have no reference from which to understand it. But the vision received by Ezekiel takes him beyond even the last example. In chapter 37, Ezekiel sees how incredibly unlikely it will be for Israel to come back as a nation, but that it will happen just the same.

> *The hand of the LORD was upon me, and carried me out in the spirit of the LORD, and set me down in the midst of the valley which was full of bones, And caused me to pass by them round about: and, behold, there were very many in the open valley; and, lo, they were very dry. And he said unto me, Son of man, can these bones live?*[4]

In this passage God is literally asking His prophet if old, dried up bones could come back to life again. He points out that *in the midst of the valley which was full of bones... there were very many... and, lo, they were very dry.* Then continuing the exchange between God and Ezekiel,

> *O Lord GOD, thou knowest. Again he said unto me, Prophesy upon these bones, and say unto them, O ye dry bones, hear the word of the LORD. Thus saith the Lord GOD unto these bones; Behold, I will cause breath to enter into you, and ye shall live: And I will lay sinews upon you, and will bring up flesh upon you, and cover you with skin, and put breath in you, and ye shall live; and ye shall know that I am the LORD.*[5]

Ezekiel does as instructed and speaks to the dried out bones the words he was given. Then in the next passage we see the results.

So I prophesied as I was commanded: and as I prophesied, there was a noise, and behold a shaking, and the bones came together, bone to his bone. And when I beheld, lo, the sinews and the flesh came up upon them, and the skin covered them above: but there was no breath in them. Then said he unto me, Prophesy unto the wind, prophesy, son of man, and say to the wind, Thus saith the Lord GOD; Come from the four winds, O breath, and breathe upon these slain, that they may live. So I prophesied as he commanded me, and the breath came into them, and they lived, and stood up upon their feet, an exceeding great army.[6]

The bones came to life and stood on their own feet. But, this only happened after the breath of life was given to them from the four winds. Now just in case Ezekiel missed the point, God spells it out for him what he has just been shown.

Then he said unto me, Son of man, these bones are the whole house of Israel: behold, they say, Our bones are dried, and our hope is lost: we are cut off for our parts. Therefore prophesy and say unto them, Thus saith the Lord GOD; Behold, O my people, I will open your graves, and cause you to come up out of your graves, and bring you into the land of Israel. And ye shall know that I am the LORD, when I have opened your graves, O my people, and brought you up out of your graves, And shall put my spirit in you, and ye shall live, and I shall place you in your own land: then shall ye know that I the LORD have spoken it, and performed it, saith the LORD.[7]

Then, a little later in the text ...

And say unto them, Thus saith the Lord GOD; Behold, I will take the children of Israel from among the heathen, whither they be gone, and will gather them on every side,

*and bring them into their own land: And I will make them
one nation in the land upon the mountains of Israel; and
one king shall be king to them all: and they shall be no
more two nations, neither shall they be divided into two
kingdoms any more at all.*[8]

The Jewish nation of ancient times was actually comprised of two states, Israel and Judah. What is especially interesting in the above text is the statement that both Judah and Israel will be united into one nation at the time when the Jews are brought back as a nation again sometime in the future, fulfilling this prophecy. Today, no longer divided into *two nations* or *two kingdoms,* the Jews are *one nation* just as God revealed to Ezekiel.

Note, also that the regaining of the "Promised Land" would be in stages. First the sinews or tendons grow on bones, then the flesh, then the skin, and finally the breath of life. This is historically what happened. First, in the beginning of the twentieth century, the Jews began to travel back to the "Promised Land." Then, in 1947, the United Nations divided a portion of land in the Middle East described as Palestine, giving the portion already dominated by the Jews there for a Jewish nation, and the other portion dominated by Arabs for an Arab state. But the Arab neighbors surrounding this newly divided land refused to accept a non-Muslim, Jewish state as their neighbor, regardless of world opinion. This led to a war in 1948 that ultimately would be called Israel's War of Independence. The Israeli victory in that war was so unlikely that many considered it a miracle. To appreciate how unlikely victory was for the Jewish forces, let's take a short look at their war for independence.

THE WAR FOR INDEPENDENCE

In 1948, the year that all out war between the Jews and Arabs broke out in Palestine, the Central Intelligence Agency estimated that the Jews of Palestine would lose their war for independence, in spite of the blessings they received from the world community. This estimate was shared by most trained observers at the time. The Arab forces in Palestine were organizing well-armed fighters that were greater in number than those on the Jewish side causing many observers to declare the fight over before it began.Military experts assumed that, even without the assistance of the various Arab countries surrounding Israel, the Palestinian Arabs outnumbered and outgunned the Jews by a wide margin. In addition, they had the support of the "Arab Liberation Army," supplying additional troops as well as artillery that the Jews did not have.[9]

When the regular army troops of the numerous hostile Arab nations were added to the mix, with their tanks, artillery, and aircraft, the chances for victory appeared nil. With a massive advantage in numbers, Arab fighters would face Jewish fighters, many of whom didn't even have a gun, or had never shot one.

The chance of Israel being reborn after over 2000 years of being *scattered among the heathen* seemed as unlikely in 1948 as ever, about as likely as old bones coming back to life. In a conversation with Moshe Sharrett, Jewish Agency Foreign Secretary, George C. Marshall, U.S. Secretary of State, informed him; "believe me, I am talking about things about which I know. You are sitting there in the coastal plains of Palestine, while the Arabs hold the mountain ridges. I know you have some arms and your Haganah (Jewish Militia), but the Arabs have regular armies. They are well trained and they have heavy arms. How can you hope to hold out?" Marshall, who only three years earlier had been instrumental in the defeat of Nazi Germany, was considered an expert on such subjects. His attitude typified the belief at the time that there was virtually no chance for the Jews to win their war for independence.

After the new state of Israel was declared on May 14, 1948, the Arab states that had threatened to invade made good on their promise and crossed the international frontier, entering the area that had been designated as part of the Jewish state by the United Nations. The Syrians moved first with Transjordan, Iraqi, and Egyptian forces quickly following their lead. Under the Egyptian command were additional forces of "Muslim Brotherhood" volunteers.[10]

Immediately after the declaration of independence by Israeli leaders, both the United States and the Soviet Union, along with most other states, recognized the new nation and cited the Arab states for their aggression. Andrei Gromyko, the Soviet delegate to the U.N. Security Council, pointed out that "this is not the first time that the Arab states, which organized the invasion of Palestine, have ignored a decision of the Security Council or of the General Assembly." These sentiments on the part of the U.S.S.R. and the United States, however, were not backed up by any actions of support such as arms or financial aid. This inaction was largely due to a belief that the Jews had little hope of winning and that, after their defeat, any arms given to them would fall into the hands of Arab forces, creating an increasingly unstable region.[11]

On July 15, 1948, after confirming that Arab forces had attacked the peaceful new Jewish state, the U.N. Security Council threatened to cite the Arab governments surrounding the Jews for aggression under the U.N. Charter. But even within the midst of this difficult time for the fledgling nation, a moment when its new life was on the verge of being extinguished, the Israel Defense Force (IDF) was created, destined to become one of the world's best fighting forces. But that glory lay in its future on that day in 1948, when most questioned if there would be a future. In the summer of that year, the United Nations sent Count Bernadotte as its representative to Palestine in an attempt to negotiate a settlement. After great efforts made on his part, with various plans proposed and repeatedly revised, the Count found he was getting nowhere. Interestingly, he noted that the Palestinian Arabs had no will of their own, nor did they ever develop any specific Palestinian nationalism. He also noted that, within their ranks, the demand for a separate Palestinian state was relatively weak. It appeared to the U.N. representative that the Palestinian Arabs would be content to simply be incorporated into Transjordan, today called Jordan.[12]

Access to the weapons necessary to fight the war would prove to be a critical advantage that the Arab forces benefited from. The United States had imposed an arms embargo over the entire area on the premise that "the Arabs might use arms of U.S. origin against Jews, or Jews might use them against Arabs," according to U.S. Undersecretary of State at that time, Robert Lovett. But this unfortunate approach did not incorporate the knowledge that the British were sending arms shipments to the Arabs. In fact, Jordan's Arab Legion was armed and trained by the British and led by a British officer. But the British support for the Arab cause was even greater than that. By the end of 1948, and the beginning of 1949, RAF airplanes were often flown by British pilots using their flying skills to attack Jewish forces on the ground. Then, on January 7, 1949, three were shot down by Israeli forces, stunning the Brits and becoming another rallying cry for the outgunned Jews.[13]

For the Jewish forces, their story was quite a different one. Most of their arms had to be smuggled in, mainly from Czechoslovakia. When Israel declared its independence it did not have a single cannon or tank, but it did have nine obsolete planes! In spite of this Arab advantage, there were signs developing on the battlefield that offered the Jews hope against the impossible odds they faced.

In a series of battles, Jewish forces began holding their own against vastly superior Arab armies. In some cases, these "rag-tag" fighters actually began defeating the stunned armies sent from her unfriendly neighbors. On May 15, about thirty Jewish defenders successfully held the Jewish town of Kfar Darom, after vastly superior Egyptian forces launched a major attack. The same thing happened at the town of Nirim, where forty-five defenders were equally successful against superior forces. In the battle of Degania, which was to become a Jewish rallying cry, improperly equipped Jewish forces defeated the regular army of Syria with small arms and Molotov cocktails.[14]

Then the first cease fire took place, successfully negotiated by the United Nations. It lasted only a month, but in hindsight would be viewed as a critical mistake for Arab forces. Believing the cease fire would allow them to increase their arms advantage Arab forces would be greatly disappointed, discovering great difficulty in obtaining them. The Israelis on the other hand took full advantage of the cease fire to recruit and train soldiers. They were also successful in bringing in large shiploads of arms primarily from Czechoslovakia. By the end of the cease fire, Arab forces suddenly found themselves outmanned and outgunned, with the Israelites now able to field approximately 60,000 fully armed troops giving them the advantage for the first time in the war.[15]

There would be another cease fire, and, then, in December 1948, the United Nations issued General Assembly Resolution 194, which called for a cessation of hostilities and a return of all refugees back to the homes from which they had been displaced. When the actual fighting finally ended in early 1949, Israel held territories beyond those set by the original United Nations plan. The Arab war to destroy Israel had failed, ironically, resulting in the Jews attaining even more land than the United Nations had offered, land considered part of the "Promised Land." But the cost to Israel was great with the loss of 6,373 Israelis, representing almost one percent of the population.[16]

Beginning on February 24, 1949, Egypt signed an armistice with Israel, followed by Lebanon on March 23, then Jordan on April 3 and Syria on July 20. Iraq simply withdrew instead of signing an armistice. The war was now over and Israel was a nation again for the first time in over 2000 years. In spite of tremendous odds, what Ezekiel prophesied long ago had actually come to pass, and with it the amazing rebirth of the ancient nation of Israel. With the fulfillment of the ancient prophecy, other words of Ezekiel's began to unfold.[17]

A TRANSFORMED LAND

In other writings from Ezekiel, he goes on to indicate that, when Israel becomes a nation again, there will be a certain transformation of the land. As he writes in chapter 36:

> *And ye shall dwell in the land that I gave to your fathers; and ye shall be my people, and I will be your God. I will also save you from all your uncleannesses: and I will call for the corn, and will increase it, and lay no famine upon you. And I will multiply the fruit of the tree, and the increase of the field, that ye shall receive no more reproach of famine among the heathen...*

> *...I will also cause you to dwell in the cities, and the wastes shall be builded. And the desolate land shall be tilled, whereas it lay desolate in the sight of all that passed by. And they shall say, This land that was desolate is become like the garden of Eden; and the waste and desolate and ruined cities are become fenced, and are inhabited. Then the heathen that are left round about you shall know that I the LORD build the ruined places, and plant that that was desolate.*[18]

In the above text, we receive a detailed description of the conditions of the land at the time of restoration and what will happen after the Jews are back.

Each of the four points indicated in the passage took place since the rebirth of Israel. It has been rebuilt and now shines as a model of modern times in an area of the world that still appears to be several centuries backward. The fields of the former desert are so prolific that what was once desolate is now farmed. A miracle of farming technology has embraced the land that was desolate prior to the rebirth of the nation. Truly, this former wasteland is now a Garden of Eden. And lastly, the "walls" protecting Israel are some of the strongest with the IDF one of the most powerful armies in the world today. All of this has come to pass since 1948.

CONCLUSION

The ancient words of Ezekiel clearly foretold the national restoration of the old Jewish state of Israel, an event that happened some 2500 years from the time in which he lived. The promised restoration took place under the most unlikely circumstances, with powerful enemies on all sides, and only a few years after the concentration camps of Nazi Germany and its fanatical leader. With their amazing victory against an array of Arab forces, some speculate if Divine intervention played a part. But this we know, the unlikely victory fulfilled a prophecy from long ago foretelling of such a restoration.

Within the ancient words are many other stories of Divine intervention on behalf of the Jews, beginning with a Pharaoh of ancient Egypt in the Book of Exodus. All of these supernatural interventions on behalf of Israel took place long ago, and are generally lost on the mind of modern man. They took place long ago because Israel did not exist for over 2000 years. So, perhaps, in a sense, with the rebirth of Israel an omen was born in 1948. If then the catastrophic events since 1991, to be reviewed here, are indicative of such an omen, and God is supernaturally acting on behalf of Israel today, then mankind could be in for a rough time in the years ahead. Especially as the Middle East "peace" process, whose ultimate goal appears to be the removal of the "Promised Land" from Israel, continues to move forward.

So, before looking at ten particular "acts of God" that have transpired since 1991, we will first look back further to the distant past. We will consider events reported to have taken place some 3,500 years ago when a nation attempted to stand between God and the fulfillment of His promise to the Israelites. In that day, the Egyptian nation was the dominant power in its region of the world, and Pharaoh ruled supreme. Yet, the ancient Hebrew Scriptures tell us that, because Pharaoh attempted to halt the fulfillment of God's promise to the Jews, Egypt fell dramatically as a nation. In looking back to these events, however, we will consider ancient records from the Egyptian side that are not widely known, but appear to be speaking about catastrophic events from the Egyptian perspective that are eerily similar to those recorded in the Book of Exodus.

CHAPTER THREE

Ancient Egypt's Defiance

The ancient Hebrew texts tell us that long ago in the land of Egypt lived Jewish slaves whose plight was hard. As a people, they had grown in numbers after their ancestor Joseph had arrived many years earlier as a slave himself. Joseph had miraculously risen in power to a seat next to Pharaoh, and, not long after his ascension, his brothers followed him to Egypt forming the foundation of the Jewish community there.

The Hebrew Scriptures also tell us that a Jewish leader named Moses received a promise from God that He would deliver the children of Israel from their bondage so that they might possess the land He was giving them. There was, however, one problem. For this promise of God to be fulfilled, Pharaoh would have to agree to release countless Jewish souls of free labor that kept Egypt running. That was a problem. Pharaoh's attempts to prevent their release would result in some of the most strange and unusual acts of God recorded in the ancient Hebrew texts. It would take those strange natural and unnatural disasters to finally convince Pharaoh that resistance against God's promise to the Jewish captives was futile. By the time Pharaoh finally acquiesced, much destruction had been visited upon his kingdom and his household. Egypt would never quite be the same again.

Now many relegate the catastrophic events said to have happened in Egypt long ago to that of a myth, a fanciful legend. But are they really just myths, or did some very strange and unusual events, recorded in the Book of Exodus, really take place? Did the Nile River actually turn into blood? Did the plague of darkness really come upon the land of Egypt? Or, were these and the other plagues metaphorically recorded representing events less unusual?

The answer to these questions may rest in the archives of the Museum of Antiquities in the Netherlands, where listed among its various catalogue entries is "Leiden 344," an ancient Egyptian papyrus written some 3500 years ago. The "Papyrus Ipuwer,"[1] as it is called, is a record of a speech of admonitions from Ipuwer, a man of obvious stature in the king's court. His words are addressing the Pharaoh of that day, and it is perhaps one of the most unusual discourses ever directed to the leader of any nation. To those familiar with the story of Exodus, his words begin to sound familiar as he discusses the terrible events that had just transpired against Egypt, and blames Pharaoh, something one did not do in those days.

This ancient papyrus, found in 1822, near the pyramids of Saqqara, paints a picture of utter destruction experienced suddenly by the Egyptian nation. The destruction is so great that violence and death, with great civil strife and a complete breakdown of civil order, appear to be the norm. Strangely, there appears to be no one around to protect the people and maintain civil order, as though the entire Egyptian army had somehow disappeared into thin air.[2] Starvation is rampant. Worst of all, something very strange has happened to the great Nile River, the lifeline of ancient Egyptian society, and now it is undrinkable.

BLOOD

In the ancient Hebrew Torah the events relating to the great exodus from Egyptian slavery are described in some detail. To convince Pharaoh to allow the Jewish slaves to leave, the Book of Exodus states,

> *...and all the waters that were in the river were turned to blood. (7:20) Then, ...and the river stank, and the Egyptians could not drink of the water of the river; and there was blood throughout all the land of Egypt.(7:21) And, ...the Egyptians digged round about the river for water to drink; for they could not drink of the water of the river.(7:24)³*

Perhaps never before has it been said that a river literally turned into blood. Such an unusual description of a river's condition would be difficult to find anywhere else in historical records. Yet, as coincidence would have it, the "Papyrus Ipuwer" records the following strange event, but this time from the Egyptian perspective.

> Plague is throughout the land. Blood is everywhere." (2:5-6) "The river is blood." (2:10) "Men shrink from tasting-human beings, and thirst after water" (2:10) "That is our water! That is our happiness! What shall we do in respect thereof? All is ruin. (3:10-13)⁴

Remember, these are translations of ancient Egyptian hieroglyphics and the term "tasting-human beings" is probably reiterating the impact on people. The Egyptian writer is clearly describing an event that has happened to the Nile River, the main source of life for Egypt. He states that it is because the river has become blood. This event represents the ruination of the river itself. Men "shrink from tasting" it, and thirst for water.

Another strange event relating to the river water is described in both the Book of Exodus as well as by the sage Ipuwer on his old papyrus. In Exodus,

> *...that thou shalt take of the water of the river, and pour it upon the dry land: and the water which thou takest out of the river shall become blood upon the dry land.(4:9)⁵*

Papyrus Ipuwer

> Behold Egypt is poured out like water. He who poured water on the ground, he has captured the strong man in misery. 7:4[6]

Here it appears that Ipuwer is observing a man who poured water on the ground, and this man has caused such a degree of trouble, that he has done great harm to the strongest men of the country. This juxtaposition of the Book of Exodus writings concerning the river of blood on the ancient Egyptian papyrus is quite strange, but, in fact, they represent only the beginning of what the old Egyptian sage wrote.

HAIL & FIRE

In the Book of Exodus we are told that Pharaoh did not give in after the first plague and so others followed. There was the plague of large hail mixed with fire that came down upon the entire land of Egypt destroying crops and causing fires. In Exodus,

> *...and the fire ran along upon the ground; and the LORD rained hail upon the land of Egypt. So there was hail, and fire mingled with the hail, very grievous...(9:23-24) ...and the hail smote every herb of the field, and brake every tree of the field.(9:25) Then, And the flax and the barley was smitten: for the barley was in the ear, and the flax was bolled.But the wheat and the rie were not smitten: for they were not grown up.(9:31-32)[7]*

As a result of the plague,

> *...and there remained not any green thing in the trees, or in the herbs of the field, through all the land of Egypt.(10:15)[8]*

The Egyptian Ipuwer describes a similar event from the Egyptian perspective:

Papyrus Ipuwer

> Forsooth, gates and columns and walls are consumed by fire."
> (2:10) "Lower Egypt weeps... The entire palace is without its
> revenues. To it belong [by right] wheat and barley, geese and
> fish (10:3-6)[9]

Here is an apparent description of the loss of revenue to Pharaoh
who would suffer since he was paid taxes in grain. Now, in a more direct
description of the loss:

Papyrus Ipuwer

> Forsooth, grain has perished on every side." (6:3) And, "For-
> sooth, that has perished which was yesterday seen. The land is
> left over to its weariness like the cutting of flax." (5:12) "Trees
> are destroyed 4:14[10]

> All animals their hearts weep. Cattle moan because of the state
> of the land (5, 5).

> Forsooth, gates columns and walls are consumed by fire;
> while the of the king's palace stands firm and endures. 7, 10[11]

It appears that the loss of grain on every side took place quickly, since
only yesterday it was still there. That eliminates drought as a possible cul-
prit and lines up with a sudden loss. There is also great distress noted in
the cattle of Egypt due to the condition of the land, and even the trees
appear to be destroyed. Interestingly, the king's palace is untouched, and
as Exodus points out, Moses would again visit there to discuss further
plagues when Pharaoh continued to resist the promise God made to the
Jewish slaves.

DARKNESS

One of the most famous plagues in the Book of Exodus was that of darkness. Darkness remained over the land for three days and was absolute, not allowing any light, even that of a candle. The Book of Exodus:

> *...that there may be darkness over the land of Egypt, even darkness which may be felt.(10:21) ...and there was a thick darkness in all the land of Egypt three days: They saw not one another, neither rose any from his place for three days...(10:22-23)[12]*

The Papyrus Ipuwer provides the following statement.

> The land is without light (9:11)[13]

Although it is a simple, one-line statement, Ipuwer is pointing out the absence of light across the land. He seems to say that there simply was no light. He did not say that most of the light was gone, or almost all light was gone, he stated that the land was without light. This would be one way to describe the plague of darkness.

The absence of light is an unusual event that would be difficult to find in any other records. In this case, it is found precisely where the Book of Exodus indicates it happened. Some try to account for this strange statement in terms of a loss of enlightenment. But, this appears to be a reach, since the statement from the Papyrus Ipuwer does not refer to any kind of enlightenment.

SPOILING OF EGYPT

After years of providing free services to their Egyptian masters, the Israelites were allowed to plunder the wealth of the Egyptians before leaving for the "Promised Land." In the Book of Exodus 12:35, we are told:

> *And the children of Israel did according to the word of Moses; and they borrowed of the Egyptians jewels of silver, and jewels of gold,*

and raiment: And the LORD gave the people favour in the sight of the Egyptians, so that they lent unto them such things as they required. And they spoiled the Egyptians.[14]

This apparently was how the Israelite slaves were repaid for their years of free service to the Egyptians. Ipuwer observes on his papyrus:

Papyrus Ipuwer

Forsooth, poor men have become the owners of good things. He who could not make his own sandals is now the possessor of riches. 2:4[15]

Gold, blue stone, silver, malachite, carnelian, bronze and Yebet stone and ... are fastened to the necks of female slaves. 3:3[16]

Behold the poor of the land have become rich, and [the possessor] of property has become one who has nothing. 8:2[17]

All female slaves are free with their tongues. When their mistress speaks, it is irksome to the servants (4, 13-14)[18]

There are several interesting ideas indicated in these passages from Ipuwer. First, those that had nothing suddenly possessed great riches. But, in a more specific description, the Egyptian sage notes that female slaves have great wealth fastened around their necks. The record of slavery throughout history indicates that this is an unusual event. Also, it is pointed out that the female slaves have become free with their tongues, something that was previously not tolerated by their masters. Apparently, something was happening that gave them courage to speak back.

FIRST BORN

The writings of Exodus note that it would take a final plague to cause Pharaoh to release the Israelites, so they might leave Egypt for the eventual fulfillment of the promise God gave them. The last plague would, by far, be the worst, leaving Egypt in grief and without strong leadership. The Book of Exodus 11:4-6:

> *And Moses said, Thus saith the LORD, About midnight will I go out into the midst of Egypt: And all the firstborn in the land of Egypt shall die, from the first born of Pharaoh that sitteth upon his throne, even unto the firstborn of the maidservant that is behind the mill; and all the firstborn of beasts. And there shall be a great cry throughout all the land of Egypt...*[19]

Perhaps, the aftermath of this last plague is being described by Ipuwer, as he recorded the following observations:

Papyrus Ipuwer

> 2:13 Every man says: we know not what has happened throughout the land

> (2, 3) Indeed men are scarce; many die and few are born. Men are few; He who places his brother in the ground is everywhere (2, 13 — 14)[20]

Ipuwer is providing a description of death on an unfathomable scale. "He who places his brother in the ground is everywhere."

Papyrus Ipuwer

> Mirth has perished and is [no longer] made. It is groaning that fills the land, mingled with lamentations (3, 13 — 14).[21]

Perhaps, the great cry foretold in Exodus is being recounted here from the Egyptian perspective:

Papyrus Ipuwer

> Forsooth, the children of princes are dashed against the walls. The offspring of desire are laid out on the high ground. Khnum

groans because of his weariness. 4:3 (Khunm was the Egyptian god of life)[22]

The children of princes represent those in high places, and it is indicated here that they have died. The "offspring of desire" are typically the first born of the Egyptian families, and here, too, they have been "laid out on the high ground." Apparently, the Egyptian god of life, Khunm,[23] had much to grieve over because so many of the young have died. It is truly a horrible time in Egypt being recorded by Ipuwer.

PILLAR OF FIRE

Once the Israelites were finally released, another strange event is described by both the Book of Exodus and the ancient Egyptian papyrus. In Exodus 13:21:

> *And the LORD went before them by day in a pillar of a cloud, to lead them the way; and by night in a pillar of fire, to give them light; to go by day and night:*[24]

Now, note within the Papyrus Ipuwer this strange observation:
Papyrus Ipuwer

> Behold the fire mounted up on high. Its burning goes forth against the enemies of the land.[25]

Ipuwer is indicating that a fire was observed high in the sky, but not at just any particular moment. Rather, this fire in the sky was observed before an enemy of the Egyptians, and is indicated, from the Egyptian point of view, as being "against" their enemy. If an army is pursuing an enemy, and observes a fire in front of their prey, they would probably see it not as the guiding force indicated in Exodus, but rather as, perhaps, coming against their enemy. In Exodus it is a guiding fire in front of the Israelites, but the Egyptians see it as against their enemy. Perhaps, the Egyptians were finally beginning to believe that their gods were coming to their rescue, after recently having fared so poorly against the God of the Israelites. Regardless, the comparison of fire in the sky, relative to an Egyptian enemy, is another quite interesting parallel between the two writings.

DEATH OF A PHARAOH

There is a town in the North Sinai of Egypt called El Arish. Its palm lined beaches along the Mediterranean make it a modern-day resort with good restaurants, hotels, and other tourist amenities. It was a town of interest to the troops of Napoleon Bonaparte in 1799, and later in the First World War by the British, who found the need to bomb it.[26] Although it should be a site of major archaeological interest, no significant archaeological projects have ever been carried out there.

There is an object of interest from ancient Egyptian times in this beautiful seaside town, which perhaps sheds light on another event recorded in the ancient Book of Exodus: the death of a Pharaoh in the Red Sea under strange circumstances. This black granite shrine, inscribed with hieroglyphics, was for years used as a cattle trough by the locals, until someone in authority decided it might be more useful within the confines of the Museum of Ismailia. In 1890, F. L. Griffith published *The Antiquities of Tell el Yahudiyeh and Miscellaneous Work in Lower Egypt during the Years 1887-1888*,[27] in which he translated the strange text on the shrine. Years later, Russian-born American independent scholar Immanuel Velikovsky would write his book *Ages in Chaos*[28] wherein he describes Griffith's translation.

The shrine text is somewhat mythological and was recorded during the Ptolemaic age, but it refers to events from a much earlier time. Some believe it records events very similar to those in the Book of Exodus concerning the fate of a Pharaoh who pursued the Israelites, and also of the plagues of locus and darkness. First, we will look at the ancient Hebrew texts that discuss the plagues of locust's and darkness, beginning with Exodus 10:5. Then, we will compare those words to the ancient Egyptian shrine. Referring to the coming locusts, the *Bible* states:

> *And they shall cover the face of the earth, that one cannot be able to see... (10:5)*

> *...and the LORD brought an east wind upon the land all that day, and all that night; and when it was morning, the east wind brought the locusts.(10:13)*

> *For they covered the face of the whole earth, so that the land was <u>darkened</u>...(10:15) (underline added)*

> *And the LORD turned a mighty strong west wind, which took away the locusts, and cast them into the Red sea...(10:19)*

> *...Stretch out thine hand toward heaven, that there may be darkness over the land of Egypt, even <u>darkness</u> which may be felt. (10:21) (underline added)*

> *...and there was a thick <u>darkness</u> in all the land of Egypt three days: They saw not one another, neither rose any from his place for three days...(10:22-23) (underline added)[29]*

What stands out during these plagues, which we are told occurred back to back to one another, was how darkness covered the land of Egypt accompanied by great wind for a period of time. The winds begin from the east bringing in the locusts that will cause, among other things, darkness across the land of Egypt *that one cannot be able to see.* The impact of the locusts over Egypt is again *that the land was darkened.* Then more wind, now from the west, to drive the locusts from Egypt as the plague ends.

But then just two verses later the plague of darkness starts; *That there may be darkness over the land of Egypt, even darkeness which may be felt.* The impact of this plague is a *thick darkness in all the land of Egypt three days. They saw not one another, neither rose any from his place for three days.* Darkness covered Egypt during the plague of locusts and then immediately following the locust was more darkness that accompanied the actual plague of darkness. Remember, that during much of this time, Egypt also experienced high winds.

Now, let's consider what is recorded on the ancient Egyptian shrine in El Arish. Here are some lines of text from the shrine:

> The land was in great affliction. Evil fell on this earth...It was a great upheaval in the residence...Nobody left the palace during nine days, and during these nine days of upheaval there was such a tempest that neither men nor gods could see the faces of their next.[30]

The shrine commemorates events of great affliction, specifically evil that "fell on this earth." Certainly, locust coming en masse from the sky could fit this fearful inscription. The shrine also indicates that, for nine days, the upheaval was so great that nobody left the palace. And quite eerily, all was so dark that the faces of those next to one were not visible. The tempest indicated on the shrine appears to match the winds associated with the bringing forth, and dispersing of the locusts, as indicated in Exodus. Both accounts indicate winds associated with an event where the sky was darkened.

Velikovsky looks at more of Griffith's translations and considers similarities between the inscriptions and the Exodus Red Sea incident, where we are told Pharaoh was killed. In the ancient Hebrew texts, the place where Moses led the Israelites was a town before the Red Sea called Pi Hahiroth. Exodus 14:2:

> ...encamp before Pihahiroth, between Migdol and the sea over against Baalzephon: before it shall ye encamp by the sea.

And a little later...

> *But the Egyptians pursued after them, all the horses and chari-*
> *ots of Pharaoh, and his horsemen, and his army, and overtook*
> *them encamping by the sea, beside Pihahiroth, before Baalz-*
> *ephon.(14:9)[31]*

The sea is, of course, the Red Sea, and it is from there that the story of the parting of the Red Sea unfolds. The Israelites find safe passage through the walls of water on either side as the army of Pharaoh pursues them. At the end of this story, the Israelites successfully reach the other shore, but Pharaoh and his army are consumed by the waters. One can only imagine the view of such an event of great waters coming back together again. Depending on how far the waters were divided, it would, no doubt, produce the greatest water show of ancient times.

Now, let's look at more of the inscriptions on the ancient Egyptian shrine of El Arish. So, after the time of great darkness, laced with a tempest (high winds), Pharaoh and his army find themselves at the following place.

Egyptian Shrine

> His Majesty--- [here words are missing] finds on this place called Pi-Kharoti.[32]

After identifying the place where Pharaoh arrives, the event that follows his arrival is explained:

> Now when the majesty of Ra-Harmachis [Harakhti?] fought with the evil doers in the pool, the Place of the Whirlpool, the evil-doers prevailed not over his majesty. His majesty leapt into the so-called Place of the Whirlpool.[33]

Velikovsky states that it is pointed out a few lines later that Pharaoh was, thrown by the whirlpool high in the air. He departed to heaven.

Velikovsky also points out that the place in Exodus called Pi Hahiroth, in Hebrew can also be spelled Pi-haKhiroth, or even Pi-Khiroth because the 'ha' is a Hebrew definite article and can be removed. It would appear that the ancient Hebrew text of Exodus and that of the Egyptian shrine are referring to the same location.

CONCLUSION

The events recorded by both Ipuwer and the El Arish Shrine relate to cataclysmic events that took place in Egypt long ago. In many ways they appear to record the same events that the Book of Exodus does, events that ancient Egypt experienced by attempting to prevent the Jews from going to the "Promised Land." Whether or not they are referring to the same events is for the reader to decide. For those of faith, the Egyptian records are probably interesting, but unnecessary. For others, however, they may raise questions not previously considered.

We live in an age where the suggestion that God would punish man on a national or even global scale, making him accountable for disobedience, is immediately dismissed by many. Yet, as the reader will see, beginning in the next chapter, disasters of an historical nature have occurred with strange commonality over the last two decades in relation to ancient warnings found in Hebrew texts. These warnings relate to land in the Middle East described as the "Promised Land" of the Jews.

As the number of natural disaster events continues to mount, coincidence should become suspect. Whether or not we have now arrived at that place is, again, for the reader to decide. But it is fair to say that the greater the number of "coincidences," the higher the probability that coincidence can be ruled out.

There is much in the ancient Hebrew Scriptures describing God's commitment of certain land to the nation of Israel, with direct and implied warnings against any nation that would molest this land to their disadvantage. (See Appendix A) Since the Jews' amazing return as a nation in 1948, after over 2000 years of being *scattered among the nations,* these Biblical warnings appear to deserve more consideration. As events since 1991 will show, recent U. S. Administrations have played the leading role in the effort to remove the "Promised Land," and the United States appears to have become the main recipient of the catastrophes detailed in chapters four through thirteen. Although the administration's efforts appear designed to promote "peace" in the region, they, none-the-less, run hard against specific promises of God to the Jews, according to the ancient Hebrew texts.

It is the current generation of mankind which must deal with any consequences of the Jews' return to Israel. Previous generations did not have this fact to deal with for almost 2000 years. Through a prophesied series of events, the Jews returned back to the land that the God of the Old Testament promised to them. Even Ezekiel appears to have provided a mathematical prophecy that unfolds until the year 1948, though it was given some 2500 years earlier (See Appendix B). Again, we see another amazing coincidence fulfilling a specific prophecy given in these old texts. It should then be reasonable to accept other ancient Jewish writings relative to the land that clearly established it as land given to them by God.

Beginning in the next chapter, the reader will see that, as leaders take actions that violate this promise, "coincidences" are taking place in the form of disasters.

It is also the current policy of various world governments, including the United States, to divide the city of Jerusalem, with a portion of it going to a new nation, Palestine. However, there are warnings covered in some detail in chapter fourteen making it clear that a price will be paid by those involving themselves in removing this land from the Jews. So having looked at the old words relating to the "Promised Land," we go back to the year 1991, and a time when then President George H.W. Bush, and his Secretary of State began the effort to remove the land from the Jews.

CHAPTER FOUR

The Perfect Storm

The President and his Secretary of State planned to leave October 28, 1991, for the Spanish capital of Madrid. The trip represented the culmination of efforts to bring together the parties to the Middle East conflict.[1] Both men believed that the peace conference, beginning in two days, represented a breakthrough that ultimately could lead to a settlement of that intractable conflict; at least, that's what they hoped. But in spite of that hope, which was shared by many who would attend the conference, the entire effort was viewed by at least one participant as a potential trap, and one that might ultimately prove hard to escape.

Israeli Prime Minister Yitzhak Shamir did not share the President's enthusiasm for the conference and would attend only to please one of the participants---the United States. He had no intention of returning even one square inch of the land Israel captured in the 1967 Six-Day War,[2] something the United States believed was necessary for peace. But for President George H.W. Bush, the catalyst for leaders from across the world agreeing to attend the conference, it would mark the high point in his administration's efforts to bring together the main players in that conflict. However, the real credit for getting to this point rested with the

President's close Texas friend, and Secretary of State, James Baker.

The process that made the Madrid Conference possible had been Baker's Herculean effort over the previous months. After logging over fifty-thousand miles traveling between the capitals of various Middle Eastern nations, Secretary Baker had achieved what few had been able to envision only a short time earlier. His efforts had seen much duplicity and back-peddling that appeared to be the negotiating norm in the Middle East, making it all the more challenging to conduct anything, let alone a conference. Years earlier, his predecessor, Henry Kissinger, had traveled to Damascus thirteen times in his efforts to forge peace, never being quite able to drain the swamp of the Middle East quagmire.[3] But Baker had no intentions of repeating that exercise in frustration. His goal was a simple one: bring together the nations of the region in a conference that would, for the first time, break the taboo of Arab countries talking peace with Israel, their implacable enemy. Although Baker knew the current political conditions in the Middle East made this conference possible, he also knew it took men like he and the President to exploit the opportunity.

* * * * * *

As Bob Case peered at his meteorological data he knew the seriousness of the situation. Having seen every type of severe weather develop over his 25-years with the National Weather Service, Case knew that what he was looking at now was unprecedented. He also knew that the forces coming together would ultimately form a monster, three distinct storm systems converging into one.[4]

Ironically, from his Boston office, he could see that New England was enjoying one of those beautiful autumn days so familiar in that part of America just prior to the onset of winter, breezy with a lot of sunshine. Although he and the other weathermen in the region had been correct about today's forecast, they could take little comfort from that success.

Case knew that the satellite images and other data presented a very different picture now, one that would unfold on the unsuspecting and peaceful coast very soon. The coast needed to be warned!

On October 28th, as the powerful and stormy weather systems converged to create the monster, it gave the appearance that the atmosphere had gone completely crazy. The three storm systems converged like three undesirable characters meeting for some unsavory purpose, creating one terrible mega-storm of incredible power and fury.[5] As Case and his weather service colleagues began the process of issuing weather advisories to the New England coastal residents, their alerts were met with some skepticism. The storm had appeared too suddenly, and the sky outside was still blue. But another aspect of the advisory stretched the imagination of the coastal residents, many of whom were familiar with the sea. It included a warning of titanic waves that the fearsome tempest might birth, waves of a terrible height, the kind usually reserved for seafaring tales told to children on rainy days along the New England Coast. But as one unfortunate sea captain and his crew were about to discover, this story was no tale.

For fishing boats along the coast, like the Andrea Gail, and her captain, Billy Tyne, there was just enough notice given to race for safe harbor before the worst of the storm would arrive, that is, if they chose to come in. But Tyne and his crew would instead remain at sea to harvest swordfish, a decision that would ultimately send them and the Andrea Gail to the deep bottom of the ocean and even deeper into seafaring lore.[6]

★ ★ ★ ★ ★ ★ ★

Sometimes events simply happen. That is to say, they happen so perfectly that no amount of planning could achieve the same result. So it was with the current Middle East climate. The conditions had fallen into place like a concerto handled by a master maestro, who, in this case, was

James Baker. The prior year, Iraqi leader Saddam Hussein had invaded Kuwait, a small but oil-rich Persian Gulf nation. In response, the United States had organized and led a coalition of nations under the banner of operation "Desert Storm,"[7] dedicated to Hussein's defeat. The coalition included a number of Middle Eastern nations which cooperated with the U.S. led effort. It was, however, the primacy of U.S. military might demonstrated on that battlefield that now leant even more significance to the fact that the United States was involved in organizing this peace conference. Prior to the Gulf War, Hussein's troops had fought for eight brutal years after invading Iran in September, 1980, and they were battle hardened. But the allied coalition of troops, led by the U.S. easily cut through the Iraqi veterans. By the end of the war, the impressive display of military might had been watched carefully by all nations in the Middle East, resulting in respect for American power reaching a new high, and the words of its leader considered with great care.

It was the dominant U.S. role in "Desert Storm" that provided the right atmosphere for its State Department to pursue a peace conference, but another significant factor presented itself on the world stage at the same time. The old Soviet Union, which had so often worked at cross purposes against the United States, had been shaken to its core by the winds of freedom sweeping Eastern Europe. Prior to the fall of the Berlin Wall,[8] it appeared that Soviet policy in the Middle East sought to cause as much trouble as possible in the region, stirring up tensions whenever the opportunity presented itself. In an area of conflict like the Middle East, the role of such an instigator nation gave it leverage by pitting factions against each other, then supplying the arms to create a client state. But in 1991, after experiencing the rumblings of democratic forces within its own borders, the Soviet Government was willing to play a constructive role in the Middle East for the first time.

All of this created the rare conditions that resulted in Baker's successful shuttle diplomacy, and the groundbreaking Middle-East peace conference that began in Madrid on October 30, 1991. Baker's efforts included visits to Cairo, Damascus, Amman, and Jerusalem twice each between September 16, and October 17. On both of his visits to Jerusalem, he had met with Palestinian representatives seeking a delegation that would represent them in Madrid. But the delegation from the Palestinian side had to be chosen with great care. The Israelis, who viewed the Palestinian Liberation Organization (PLO) as a terrorist group, with the blood of many innocent Israelis on its hands, refused to have any dealings with it. The PLO had distinguished itself in the infamous massacre of Israeli athletes at the 1972 Munich Olympics.[9] Any Israeli government caught dealing with the PLO would be viewed as having granted it legitimacy and would place itself in real trouble with the nation's political right. For Baker, this Israeli requirement, that no PLO members attend the conference, would be another obstacle he would have to overcome, since Yasser Arafat's organization had become the main rallying point for the goals and aspirations of the Palestinian people. Ultimately, a Jordanian-led, Palestinian delegation, with no overt ties to the PLO, would be chosen.

* * * * * * *

In late October, as the warm days of summer drift away to a memory, the first signs of winter begin their icy march south from Canada. Meteorologists, dutifully mindful to keep an eye on the weather of that colorful month, fasten themselves to the tools of their trade, tracking the movement of weather patterns, allowing them to perform their craft with some degree of accuracy. Gratefully, to the benefit of the forecasters, there appear to be certain weather patterns that repeat themselves time and again. The convergence of three storm systems into one, however, is not one of them.

The first storm was a low pressure system that developed over the Great Lakes, and proceeded to follow the usual path of North American weather:

west to east, from Chicago to Maine, and on past Nova Scotia. As it was traveling along this path, it met another piece of weather energy, an icy cold high-pressure system moving down from Canada. These two systems then combined into one storm off the Nova Scotia coast. The third, and final, piece of this weather puzzle, was the late season hurricane Grace that was moving north. Instead of these diverse and powerful weather systems canceling one another out, they combined into a system that exploded in both size and energy. After studying the circumstances of such a combination, Case would call it the "Perfect Storm." The name would stick.

The Perfect Storm would not follow the west-to-east tendency of northern hemisphere weather systems, coming from the Midwest and then moving east and out over the north Atlantic. Instead, having formed far out to sea, the Perfect Storm would add to its reputation by engaging in what weather professionals call "retrogression," moving from the east to the west. Without this reversal from the typical tract, it could not have impacted the New England coast. Now with this rare retrogression spanning a 1000 mile trek, the fortunes of the New England coast reversed with it.[10]

* * * * * * *

Without U. S. leadership, the Middle East peace conference could never have taken place, even in so positive an environment. As the only superpower on Earth, no other nation had the clout to convene such a conference, especially considering that the warring parties were not even on speaking terms. The gathering in Madrid would include representatives from Israel, Syria, Lebanon, and Egypt, as well as the Jordanian-Palestinian delegation. It would also have very heavy security. The main thrust of the effort was to get the parties to begin talking to one another. The talk's goal was to ultimately lead to the fulfillment of the United Nations Resolutions requiring Israel to trade "territory for peace," as President Bush would state.

The central belief behind the conference was that peace would be achieved if the lands captured by Israel in 1967 were returned. For the Syrians it meant the return of the Golan Heights. For the Palestinians it meant the West Bank, known to Israelis as Judea and Samaria. All of these lands, according to the ancient Hebrew Scriptures, were a part of the "Promised Land" foretold by Ezekiel. In exchange for the "Promised Land," assurances of Israel's right to exist would be granted from the various mortal enemies that surrounded her, along with diplomatic recognition.

The U.N. passed the two resolutions in November, 1967, Security Council Resolutions 242 and 338.[11] They were adopted shortly after the famous 1967 Six-Day War where Israel, as in olden times, had defeated the combined foreign armies of Egypt, Syria, and Jordan. Outmanned and outgunned, and sensing that her enemies were about to attack, Israel launched a preemptive, lightning strike, that succeeded quicker than anyone dared to imagine, capturing large tracts of land from all three nations. Due to their proximity to Israel, these lands had previously been used as launching pads for attacks against the Jewish state. Now they were under Israeli control again for the first time in over 2000 years.

Included in this victory was Jerusalem, the city that was every Middle East negotiator's nightmare. Spoken of jealously by God in the Hebrew Scriptures, it is the city that Judaism, Christianity, and Islam all revere. The foundation of the U.N. resolutions required Israel to return the land acquired in the Six-Day War, including East Jerusalem, even though the lands seized were from nations that had attempted, on more than one occasion, to "drive her into the sea." During a previous attempt to destroy Israel, in 1948, the combined Arab forces had failed to defeat the much smaller Israeli armed forces. Then at the conclusion of the Six-Day War in 1967, the treasure trove of land taken from Jordan, Syria, and Egypt became the new Arab justification for the ongoing conflict. Except for the Sinai, the lands acquired from this war were indicated in the ancient Hebrew writings of Ezekiel as given to Israel by God. Within captured Judea was the town of Bethlehem, the birth place of Jesus, and Bethany, where Jesus raised Lazarus from the dead. Also included in Judea was Qumran, the ancient Jewish village, where the Dead Sea Scrolls were found. Now, in 1991, events had come together for a push by Israel's strongest and best friend in the world to bring the Jewish state to the negotiating table, with the "Promised Land" the main bargaining chip.

Kenneth Stein of Emery University, one of those responsible on the U.S. side for setting up the conference, noted:

> The Madrid Peace Conference was an American planned conference in which the Soviets played only a supporting role. The conference's formulation, conduct, and diplomatic aftermath reaffirmed the role of the United States over the Soviet Union in the region.[12]

So tenuous was the Soviet Union's situation, that months after the conference was over, it would lie on the "ash heap of history," as former President Reagan had once predicted was certain to happen. With the United States as the only superpower, and the end of Soviet meddling, it appeared that progress might be made after all.

The Madrid Peace Conference represented a major breakthrough in the region, because for the first time, it gathered together the various parties associated with the conflict, allowing them to finally talk face-to-face. The ultimate goal of the conference was the return of lands captured in the 1967 conflict. To many in Israel, and around the world, the seizure of these lands was taken as a sign of the further fulfillment of Ezekiel's prophetic utterances from so long ago. But to the international community, the captured land was one big headache. In the initial war against the Jews, the Arab nations surrounding Israel had warned against their impending declaration of nationhood, even though the plan approved by the United Nations included the creation of an Arab state alongside a Jewish one. Then, on May 14, 1948, when David Ben-Gurion declared the independent state of Israel, the 1948 Palestinian war entered its second phase, with the intervention of several Arab armies the following day attacking the new nation of Israel.

Somehow, the tiny Jewish army defeated the combined Arab armies against fantastic odds that again led many to believe that their nationhood was from the hand of God. The prophecy of Ezekiel, given some 2500 years earlier, had been fulfilled. But against this prophetic backdrop, the United States was engaging all of its financial, military and diplomatic might to pressure Israel into giving up the land.

As the Madrid Peace Conference convened, it did so in the ultimate pursuit of United Nations Resolutions 242 and 338, requiring Israel to relinquish the lands acquired in the 1967 war. This pitted both the Madrid Conference, and the United States of America on a collision course with a promise to the Jews from God Himself. In spite of the good intentions of seeking "peace," success for the Madrid Conference would mean that God's promise to the Jews would be reversed by mankind.

As October 30th began, with the doors to the conference finally opening, the attendees met at the Spanish Royal Palace in the city of Madrid. The Spanish government, hoping to add its own impact to the proceedings, thought the kingly splendor of the 2800-room site would bring out the more regal side in the participants. Built at the end of the 9th century, it had originally been constructed as a fortress. Then, in the 14th century, after being gutted by fire, it acquired the trappings of a royal residence during the restoration. As the attendees entered its opulent splendor, and the historical conference began, events of a different nature began unfolding on the other side of the Atlantic Ocean.

★ ★ ★ ★ ★ ★ ★

The storm's fury on October 30th brought sustained high winds of at least 70 mph. Buoys reporting off the coast of Long Island showed that the wind was whipping up 40 to 80-foot waves across the North Atlantic. Other buoys reporting off of the Nova Scotia coast recorded higher winds and a wave that reached a height of 101 feet!

Bob Case would later be quoted as saying it was an unprecedented set of circumstances that caused the "Perfect Storm" to develop, to "explode to epic proportions and then head for the coast. If any of the components were out of sync, the epic storm would not have happened." Case would conclude: "You were looking at a set of meteorological circumstances that come together maybe every 50-100 years."[13]

As the attendees began shaking hands to begin the Madrid conference on October 30, 1991, the worst that the "Perfect Storm" had to offer was delivered against the bewildered New England coastal towns. Waves of 30 to 40-feet began striking the shore. As President Bush was in Madrid delivering the opening remarks to the conference, Kennebunkport, Maine was being slammed by a 30 foot wave that crashed over the President's house located there, causing severe damage. The first floor, ripped open by the raging sea, exposing the family sitting room, a bedroom, and the living room, the furious waves sending the Bush furniture into the ocean.[14][15]

Scientists that studied this storm stated that its formation and retrogression made it a "freak of nature." This "freak of nature" struck just as the Madrid Peace Conference was beginning on the other side of the ocean. With the conference's ultimate purpose to remove from the Israelites a portion of the "Promised Lands," was the storm's timing just a coincidence? It would easily be considered such, if the story stopped here. But the story does not end here with the "Perfect Storm;" it only begins.[16]

CHAPTER FIVE

Hurricane Andrew

I t had been less than a year since the titanic waves birthed by the "Perfect Storm" had spent their last moments terrorizing the seafaring communities along the New England coast. Although that storm had blown its last mighty gusts the previous October, it was now the Madrid Peace effort that was a force to be reckoned with.

After the first gathering at Madrid, the peace process had resulted in several more meetings, but with no substantial results. The obstacle to making "progress" was Israeli Prime Minister Yitzhak Shamir. Shamir, no "peace" dove, did not believe that the "land for peace" idea would work, and was unwilling to risk Israel's security to find out. Should Israel return lands repeatedly used as launching pads for attacks against her in the past, he would reason, she would once again become highly vulnerable to the multitude of enemies surrounding her. He knew that unlike her Arab enemies, to lose one war meant the end of the nation. But the public in Israel had grown weary of the constant state of tension that Israel seemed to exist within. So, in the next election, Shamir was repudiated, with the voters giving the Prime Minister's office to Yitzhak Rabin, widely viewed as more accommodating to the peace process.

The new Israeli Prime Minister had become an illustrious character in the young nation. He was a central figure in Israel's War for Independence, and was a significant leader during its first five decades as a nation. It was largely due to his efforts that the Israeli Defense Forces became one of finest and most effective fighting machines in the world. But Rabin's beliefs had morphed considerably over the years. So much so, that upon becoming Prime Minister in 1992, he concluded that land was not as important as peace, and truly believed that giving it up would buy Israel peace with her Muslim neighbors.

This represented a sharp break from the more traditional belief that the land was given to Israel by God Himself. By embracing such new views, Rabin created a wide gulf between himself and his fellow countrymen. Many of his fellow citizens also believed the land was absolutely necessary for the very survival of the Jewish nation. Many would conclude that trading "land for peace" would not only violate God's will, but place the nation's very existence at risk.

But Rabin was convinced otherwise, believing that the greater threat to Israel's future was a lack of true peace. In his book, *Soldier of Peace: The Life of Yitzhak Rabin*,[1] Dan Kurzman points out that, later in his term of office, Rabin decided to unilaterally withdraw from Gaza and much of the West Bank territory, ignoring the many violations of previous peace agreements by the Palestinians. But now, as Rabin approached the 6th round of the Madrid Middle East peace process, he had every intention of cooperating with the U.S. push to swap "land for peace."

* * * * * * *

As the planet's tilt toward the sun favors the northern hemisphere, the seas become fertile hatching grounds for storms to develop from the coast of West Africa, to the Caribbean. Much of their fierce potential is drawn from the rainy season on the West Coast of Africa, causing that part of the world to be eyed with care by weather experts in the United States. In years past, before the time of "weathermen," unfortunate travelers on the high seas took their chances between the months of June and September, with the bottom of the sea testifying to their outcome. Like a prize fighter telegraphing his next punch, the waters off West Africa often tell the weathermen what is heading for the United States coast well before it arrives. It is that same African coast where our story begins.

On August 14th, 1992, as the final plans for the upcoming peace conference, now to be held in Washington, were being completed, clouds began coalescing over the West Africa nation of Senegal. The disturbance, so common for that coastal nation during its hot summer months, would soon become better organized, developing into a tropical wave that soon began moving westward. For the next several days meteorologists from the Miami National Hurricane Center would watch the system carefully for direction and any signs of strengthening. By August 19th, the system would be christened Tropical Storm Andrew.[2]

The 1992 hurricane season had been deceptively quiet thus far, lessening the sense of caution Florida coastal residents should have during the threatening months. But there was another factor adding to this sense of complacency. Not since Hurricane Donna in 1960, and Hurricane Betsy, five years later, had south Florida suffered a direct hit from a powerful storm. Neither of those storms even hit the mainland, instead striking the vulnerable Keys. In fact, it had not been since 1947 that a major storm made landfall on a mainland south Florida beach. That storm had attained wind speeds of 160 mph striking the Pompano Beach area with devastating force. But few remembered it, and even fewer expected Florida to experience anything like it again. Since the 1947 storm, millions of people had moved to South Florida, and few of these residents were prepared to experience a direct hit from a storm, especially a powerful one.[3]

As diligent weathermen across the Florida coast watched, measured, and projected the storms expected path across the Atlantic, it began to appear that this threat, too, would come to nothing. On August 20th, as Andrew continued to move northwesterly, it encountered strong wind shear in the upper atmosphere and began to weaken, its winds dropping to only 45 mph. Now, with its path more northerly and its winds downgraded, it appeared once again that the Florida coast would be spared. But that would soon change.[4]

* * * * * * *

The fundamental change Rabin brought to Israeli policy made the sixth round of the Madrid process unique. In September 1992, the *Seattle Times* ran an article titled "Land for Peace---Rabin Puts Golan Heights On The table With Syria." The article noted the difference in Rabin's approach, compared to his predecessor's:

> June election of Prime Minister Yitzhak Rabin is a potent example of the difference a change in leadership can make. Rabin has uttered the words that never would have crossed his predecessor's lips: Israel is open to returning the strategic Golan Heights to Syria in exchange for real peace.[5]

These words, and others like them from Rabin, brought about a vocal and harsh reaction against him from significant elements of the Israeli population. Using the benefit of hindsight, a *USA Today* article in November 2008, would reflect back on 1992:

> ...hard liners branded the Israeli leader (Rabin) a traitor for proposing to hand over land to the Palestinians in exchange for peace. Some extremist rabbis called for his death, and leaders of the hawkish Likud Party addressed a tumultuous Jerusalem demonstration featuring posters of Rabin in a Nazi SS uniform.[6,7]

There could be no greater insult for a Jewish leader of Israel, than to be depicted as a Nazi. It appeared that the nerve struck in his opponents by Rabin's new "land for peace" approach, was now being returned.[8] As round six of the Madrid Conference began, the shift in Israeli foreign policy toward "land for peace" placed the Prime Minister of Israel and the United States on the same page. According to the ancient Hebrew Scriptures, both were on a collision course with God.

★ ★ ★ ★ ★ ★

Jim and Tonya had married late the previous year and were enjoying life as newlyweds near the south Florida coast. With Tonya carrying their first child, the couple had determined that their new home in Homestead was a good fit for their growing family. But, on August 21st, they noticed reports on the news that the hurricane, which until very recently appeared as no threat to them, was now strengthening. It appeared that the wind shear that had worked so effectively against it was no longer a factor, allowing the warm waters beneath the storm to work their dark magic. Even more disturbing, it became apparent that the storm's track had also changed, now moving due west, directly on course for south Florida.

As weather reports continued following the storm's progress, their tone grew more ominous by the hour. By noon the next day, August 22nd, wind speeds had gone from 45 to 80 mph, once again reaching hurricane strength. By the next morning, the news of the hurricane's strengthening over night presented a shocking wake-up call to the residents of Homestead, as sustained wind speeds had increased to a powerful 120 mph. Now, with nothing but warm water between the hurricane and the coast, even more strengthening was projected. Quite suddenly the Florida coast was threatened, and would very soon be hit.[9]

Governor Lawton Chiles declared a state of emergency in the three counties of Monroe, Dade and Broward in south Florida, sending more than 700,000 residents fleeing to higher ground.[10] As Jim and Tonya contemplated what to do, they decided to ride it out. Confident everything would be alright, Jim did not even bother to board up the windows. Originally from New York and looking for work, he had moved to the Sunshine state where he and Tonya met. He had heard about hurricanes, watching them on the news, but had never known anyone that had been through one. As he watched the news reports announcing the growing threat, the reality of what it represented had been lost on him. As the hours of Sunday, August 23rd ticked away, the opportunity to leave slipped away. For those that decided to remain, the voices of various weathermen in the region would be the only contact they would have with the outside world during the frightening hours soon to arrive. One of those voices was Brian Norcross, of the local CBS affiliate, who would be credited with "talking the people through it."[11]

With the storm continuing to strengthen, and heading directly for Homestead, the evening of the 23rd was one of last-minute preparations. One of those preparations was an idea that came from Norcross, urging all residents that remained to identify the safest room in the house. The "safe room," as it was appropriately called, would most likely be a bathroom or even a closet. Because those rooms were usually the smallest in the house or apartment, the concentration of the wood frame supporting it would provide the greatest protection in the event of a structural collapse. Along with that recommendation, Norcross suggested having a mattress in the safe room for protection from high speed flying objects. Both pieces of advice would save lives during the terrifying evening soon to come. The storm would arrive at 4 A.M., only a few hours away.[12]

* * * * * * *

In preparation for an eventual abandonment of a portion of the "Promised Land," Rabin stated during a press conference with President Bush that the building of settlements in the territories in question would be stopped or cancelled. Bush, adding his approval, stated that the Prime Minister's actions "took a lot of courage." The president should have been pleased, and he was. It had been his administration's policy to pursue a Middle East peace by trading land, a policy he hoped would eventually result in Israel returning all of the lands captured in 1967.[13][14] On August 24th, 1992, the Madrid Peace Conference would continue in Washington, D.C. with all of the major parties in attendance. With the talks in Washington, U. S. diplomats were now in a position to apply the maximum pressure on Israel to pursue the "land for peace" policy that the previous Shamir Administration had refused.[15] Unlike the previous conferences, the United States would now have a willing participant in the new Israeli government under Rabin.

A spokeswoman for the Syrian government that participated in the negotiations would reminisce weeks later of the difference in the new Israeli attitude, noting how much more accommodating it was compared to the previous Likud government's attitude under Shamir. She noted a "different style" existed in the Israeli delegation with Israeli statements representing a change from the prior government's positions. The most striking difference was that they acknowledged the principal of "land for peace."[16] This was a huge difference from the previous Israeli government's position, and it pleased a Bush administration that had been frustrated with Shamir's refusal to make such a trade. As a result of the new Israeli attitude, President Bush announced that the U.S. Treasury would provide guarantees to allow Israel to obtain, on favorable terms, credits worth US $10 billion from private U.S. banks. Under the previous, less cooperative Israeli government of Shamir, these same loans had been refused.[17]

* * * * * * *

As the morning hours of Monday, August 24th arrived, Jim and

Tonya could tell the winds had significantly increased. Tonya, beginning to fear that the decision to stay was a big mistake, headed for the safe room which was a closet on the second floor, bringing inside the mattress Norcross had advised. Then she heard something explode. At first the explosions near the house were as inexplicable as they were frightening to the couple. Jim, peering out of a window, could see that as electrical transformers in the neighborhood were struck by the powerful winds, they would explode. Although that explained the explosions, it did not bring any comfort. When the eye of the storm finally approached land-fall, the intensity of the winds increased with a fearsome roar that would continue for the next two hours. With the storm's full fury now striking, the terrifying sound of the house tearing apart could be heard.

The National Hurricane Center, located just a few miles from the center of the storm was dealing with a problem of their own. The Center found itself at a disadvantage in attempting to determine how strong the force of wind had become. After recording sustained winds of 164 mph, their measuring equipment was destroyed. Turning then to a buoy located just off the coast, they recorded a gust of 169-mph, until it, too, was destroyed. Now essentially blinded by the powerful force striking them, the National Hurricane Center had one last source remaining for detailed information on the might of the storm. Reconnaissance aircraft, continuing to fly their daring missions into the bands of Andrew, relayed critical data to weather officials throughout the stormy night. Their instruments recorded sustained winds of 160-165 mph with gusts to 200 mph![18] As those powerful winds raged across the coast, Jim and Tonya raced downstairs to their second safe room, the bathroom, which would prove to be a critically good decision. As the sound of the house coming apart grew, they crawled inside the tub. Jim covered his wife and unborn child and then placed the mattress over all of them. They would survive. But Homestead and the surrounding area would not, suffering devastation on an unimaginable scale.

* * * * * * *

On August 24th, as the President officially opened Round Six of the Madrid Peace Conference just hours earlier, Hurricane Andrew had finished ripping through south Florida like a gigantic saw in the hands of a madman. The President would be distracted that morning as he met the dignitaries attending the conference, his attention drawn to reports streaming into the White House describing the magnitude of what had just struck the United States. The carefully choreographed gathering in Washington D.C. would be disrupted, having to continue without the President that evening. Instead, he would fly in a helicopter over south Florida, awestruck by the devastation inflicted earlier in the day. Andrew would rank 4th in all-time severity behind three storms infamous in their own day: 1935 hurricane that hit the Florida Keys, 1969's Camille, and of more recent notoriety, 2005's Katrina.[19] In the frightening dark of night, Hurricane Andrew brought a wall of water over 16-feet high on shore. When morning came, it was discovered that the storm had placed large boats one atop the other as if nature had played some morbid game overnight. Its winds possessed such force that cars and trucks were temporarily suspended in mid-air, moved at will by its invisible arms in an unbelievable sight for those unlucky enough to witness. It is considered one of the worst natural disasters in U.S. history, with over $30 billion in damages. But even that cost didn't begin to measure the toll on those that lived through it. Some never recovered. A staggering 162,000 houses and businesses sustained major damage or were destroyed. Tens of thousands would sadly join the ranks of the homeless.

But the cost of the storm for President Bush would continue to mount well beyond that fateful day in August. Pentagon officials would later report they were ready to deliver large amounts of emergency aid to the stricken area, but failed to do so because the President did not request it. For Jim and Tonya, and the countless souls languishing without food or water in the Florida sun, Federal aid would not arrive until Thursday, three days later.[20] As the storm's victims began to lash out at the Bush administration for the delay, excuses given by his supporters seemed hollow. The image of the president had been damaged. He was accused of being too focused on foreign affairs at the expense of the domestic needs of the nation.[21] In the Presidential election, held just two months later, the Clinton campaign would successfully exploit this image problem in an election that Bush was destined to lose.

The historically severe nature of Andrew made it unique among storms, adding itself as the second "coincidence," relative to efforts to reverse a specific promise from God, according to the ancient Hebrew Scriptures. [22]

CHAPTER SIX

The Great Flood

After decades of blood, hate, and fear, the Madrid Peace process represented a noble effort on the part of the United States to be peace maker in the Middle East conflict. Indeed, the efforts of the U. S. in this regard were unmatched, if for no other reason than as the only superpower on Earth, no other nation had the clout to attempt to untie that tangled web of conflict. Fourteen years earlier, in 1979, the prodding of President Carter eventually led Egypt and Israel to sign a peace treaty. In an administration starved for a foreign policy success, the Camp David Peace Accord was recognized by the world community as a significant achievement for world peace.[1]

Years later the first President Bush would initiate the Madrid Middle East Peace process in October 1991, with the hope of creating a basis for a solution between the warring parties. As one of the tools of pressure at his disposal, Bush withheld $10 billion in loan guarantees for Israel when then Israeli Prime Minister Shamir appeared to be an obstacle to the process of "land for peace," according to the will of the U.S. administration. Not only was Shamir opposed to trading land, but he had adamantly refused to have any dealings with Arafat, whose hands had been stained by the blood of many innocent Jews slaughtered by his group over the years. Not until the next Israeli elections, and the elevation of Yitzhak Rabin to the Prime Minister's office, did the Madrid peace process begin to move forward.

Not long after Hurricane Andrew devastated the Florida coast, Bill Clinton, the Democratic nominee, won the presidential election. Six months after that election, in April 1993, the new Clinton administration would pick up the peace baton of Madrid announcing that the process would resume after months of lying dormant.[2] The effort would include familiar faces from the previous conferences, including representatives from both Israel and the Palestinians. However, this time something else was also taking place, something entirely unexpected.[3]

Sometimes things are best done in secret, reducing critical eyes and lips to hindsight. Ironically, such a time was found by common antagonists who could agree on little else, but did agree to be secret. Unknown to the other participants at the conference, Israeli and Palestinian representatives were simultaneously meeting, incognito, in Oslo, Norway, under the mediation of that nation's Prime Minister.[4] It was here in secret that both sides could focus on issues without critics at home assaulting them in public. It was here that the breakthrough came.

* * * * * * *

Five hundred years is a very long time. Five hundred years ago the New World had just been discovered. Yet, for the Midwest United States the events that would take place in the summer of 1993 are thought by some to only happen every five hundred years; and it all began on a rainy day.[5]

Throughout North America, as the winter months finally exhort their last efforts for snow, sending to the sidewalks an army of weary snow shovelers hoping the last of the white powder has fallen, the month of April begins. When the snow melts and the rains come, the two collude to swell the great Mississippi river, sometimes to the limit of man's efforts to contain it.

As April 1993 began, negotiations between the Israelis and Palestinians that would ultimately lead to an agreement for the removal of a portion of the "Promised Land," were underway. Meanwhile, the Midwest United States began receiving steady rainfall. The National Weather service had predicted "below normal precipitation for the coming summer" the month before, but was alert to the potential for flooding should rainfall reach above average levels. In the previous year the ground in the Midwest had become saturated, and so the hope was for normal amounts of rainfall during 1993.[6]

But an unusual set of climate circumstances had become established over the entire region effectively fueling continuous rains. The Bermuda High, a high pressure system which typically sits out in the Atlantic Ocean during the summer months and steers hurricanes toward the United States, was stronger than normal and had moved farther to the north and west. The result was a dam of air that stopped storms dead in their tracks over the Midwest, not allowing them to move off to the East Coast to deposit some of their showers.[7] The end result of this highly unusual atmospheric circumstance would be a deluge of almost Biblical proportions.

* * * * * * *

Beyond the secrecy aspect of the negotiations, part of the reason for the breakthrough between the Israelis and Palestinians in Oslo was the weakened Palestinian position. With the collapse of the Soviet Union, its superpower backing was gone. Then there was Iraq. Arafat had made the mistake of backing Hussein during the Gulf Crisis of 1990, the end result being an alienation of the financially powerful Gulf States Iraq had threatened. Also, along with the collapse of the Soviet Union came a mass exodus of Jews from that part of the world. With these new immigrants streaming into Israel, a place was needed to put them, and the territories of Judea and Samaria beckoned. This created further motivation for the Palestinians to negotiate some kind of an agreement that might slow or stop the settlements.[8]

On the Israeli side, a different motivation convinced it to finally make a deal. Over the years Israeli governments had gotten the gist of what the United States was expecting from them, especially in regard to the "land for peace" swap that was suppose to bring peace to the region. They also knew that not "cooperating" with a U.S. Administration could spell trouble in the most important relationship Israel had in the world. Shamir had discovered this the hard way with the loan guarantee issue. Now, U.S. influence over Israel had become so powerful that the Arab American Institute President, James Zogby, looked to pressure Israel through Washington, instead of Jerusalem. As one of the foremost Israeli detractors in the United States, he declared that "the battleground for Middle East peace is as much here in Washington, and Congress, as it is in the Middle East." So when Israel and the Palestinians announced that they had come to an agreement, it was not surprising that they had the blessings of the United States, even though the U.S. was not directly involved in those particular negotiations.[9] Nor was it any surprise that the agreement would be signed in Washington D.C.

The journey to an agreement between the bitter foes had begun in April 1993. In May of that year, Israeli Foreign Minister Shimon Peres had called Joel Singer, a legal advisor to the Israeli Foreign Ministry, asking him to review some preliminary proposals worked out by Israeli and PLO negotiators the month before, in April. For Singer, that began a three-month shuttle between Jerusalem and Oslo, Norway, until the two sides came to an agreement. Recalling the moment when Peres handed an advance text of the agreement to Secretary of State Christopher, Singer observed "His lower jaw dropped and for the first, and last time in my life, I saw Warren Christopher smile." The Israelis had pleased the U.S. administration. Knowing that the agreement is what the United States wanted from Israel, the offer was made to present it as an American document.[10] But Christopher declined, instead settling for the agreement to be signed at the White House with the United States as a signer along with Russia. Christopher's refusal to claim it as an American document was on the technicality that the U.S. had not literally negotiated it. Although technically true, all parties familiar with the agreement knew it was what the U.S. wanted. Israel had gotten the message.

Shortly before the Madrid conference was set to begin, Christopher reiterated that U.S. official policy was for a process that involved, as its central principal, the notion of "land for peace." According to UN Security Council Resolutions 242 and 338, the belief held that true peace could be achieved if only the land was returned.[11]

The U.S. position was not lost on the Israeli negotiators as they met in Oslo. It was the same "land for peace" effort that Israeli Prime Minister Rabin had embraced in August 1992, during the sixth round of Madrid. This policy, however, was squarely in opposition to the ancient Hebrew Scriptures that had foretold the return of the land to the Jews. Now, another attempt was being made to alter God's promise, if not reverse it.

* * * * * * *

As April turned into May and the rains continued, flooding began to appear in various parts of the U.S. mid-section. By the end of June the first dams began to burst, submerging 100 homes to their rooftops on the Black River in Western Wisconsin. In the upper 200 miles of the Mississippi River, locks and dams were unable to operate, and soon that section of the mighty river became closed to traffic.

The rains continued. Soon bridges over the Mississippi River were out, or not accessible from Iowa to Missouri, due to instability caused by the onslaught of rushing waters.[12] Homeowners throughout the Midwest began filling sandbags in an effort to save their towns and homes along the expanding rivers and tributaries. Before it was all over, 26.5 million sandbags would be made during the summer of 1993.

As June and July turned into August, the damage became breathtaking. By September, when the flooding began to subside, 40 of 229 federally built levees had been overtopped or damaged. Non-federal levees fared even worse; 1043 damaged or overtopped out of 1347! Barge traffic on both the Mississippi and Missouri Rivers was halted for almost two months, ten commercial airports flooded, and all railroad traffic in the Midwest was halted. Both the 1993 and 1994 harvests were lost in the afflicted nine states. [13][14]

★ ★ ★ ★ ★ ★ ★

On September 13, 1993, at a ceremony on the South Lawn of the White House, the United States hosted the signing of the historical "peace accord" between Israel and the Palestinians. After months of negotiations, the parties came to an agreement on August 20. This represented the first agreement between the Israelis and Palestinians toward ending the conflict, and sharing the holy land between the Jordan River and the Mediterranean Sea that both claimed as their homeland. Israeli Foreign Minister Shimon Peres, and PLO foreign policy official Mahmoud Abbas, signed the "Declarations of Principals on Interim Self Government Arrangements." President Clinton, presiding over the ceremony, pointed out in his remarks:

> Two years ago in Madrid, another President took a major step
> on the road to peace by bringing Israel and all her neighbors to-
> gether to launch direct negotiations. And today we also express

our deep thanks for the skillful leadership of former President George Bush. Mr. Prime Minister [Rabin Israel], Mr. Chairman [Arafat Palestinians], I pledge the active support of the United States of America to the difficult work that lies ahead.[15]

And, indeed, United States policy would continue to be one of active engagement. The accord was landmark in that it envisaged Israel engaging in a process of transferring portions of the West Bank and Gaza Strip to the control of an interim governing entity called the Palestinian Authority. In the presence of more than 3000 onlookers, President Clinton witnessed the amazing scene of Palestinian leader Yasser Arafat, and Israeli Prime Minister Rabin, old and bitter enemies, sealing the agreement with a handshake. Rabin, a former Chief-of-Staff of the Israeli Defense Forces, spoke movingly:

> We the soldiers who have returned from the battle stained with blood; we who have seen our relatives and friends killed before our eyes; we who have fought against you, the Palestinians; we say to you today in a loud and clear voice: Enough of blood and tears. Enough!

Arafat, a guerrilla leader who for years had been hunted by Israeli forces, declared that, "The battle for peace is the most difficult battle of our lives. It deserves our utmost efforts because the land of peace yearns for a just and comprehensive peace."[16][17]

Middle East history had been made, with an event that was only exceeded by the Camp David accord of 1979. Since becoming the Prime Minister, Rabin had been the first since the Sinai deal to truly push the idea of "land for peace." The whole concept of "land for peace" was one that completely defied the beliefs of various religious factions within the Israeli Knesset, or parliament, which was assured by the ancient words that the lands being traded had been given to Israel by God Himself. But now, for the first time, a process for removing these lands had been placed in "peace" accords signed by an Israeli leader. In return, Israel received acknowledgement of its right to exist from Arafat and the PLO, a right the Israeli Defense Forces had been guaranteeing since 1948.[18]

* * * * * * *

The National Weather Service would eventually declare the 1993 Midwest flood "one of the most significant and damaging natural disasters ever to hit the United States."[19] As dramatic as that statement was, it was no exaggeration: "The flood was unusual in the magnitude of the crests, the number of record crests, the large area impacted, and the length of the time the flood was an issue." The magnitude of the flood was overwhelming, severely impacting nine Midwestern states. Incredibly, over 600 river forecast points in the Midwestern United States were above flood stage at the same time. In total, nearly 150 major rivers and tributaries were impacted, representing the largest and most significant flood event ever to occur in the United States.[20] Tens of thousands of people were evacuated from their homes along the range of the destruction, with many never to return again. About 20 million acres of farmland were inundated, impacting its usability for years to come. The amounts of rainfall in the eastern Dakotas, southern Minnesota, eastern Nebraska, Wisconsin, Kansas, Iowa, Missouri, Illinois, and Indiana would eventually reach between 200 and 350 percent of what was considered normal for the summer months.

The critical factor in the disaster was the continuous nature of the rainfall, with many locations in the nine-state area experiencing rain twenty days or more in the month of July. The Great Flood of 1993, as it would later be called, was fed by rainfall to produce flooding that exceeded 500-year recurrence intervals. In plain English, it was a very, very rare natural disaster. Within the nine impacted states, 400,000 square miles were covered by the flood for an extremely long duration of nearly 150 days. In Kansas City, 810 of 810 non-federal levees failed.

Over a hundred years ago Mark Twain said of the Mississippi River, it:

> cannot be tamed, curbed or confined.....you cannot bar its path with an obstruction which it will not tear down, dance over and laugh at.[21]

In the summer of 1993, the Mississippi drove home the famous writer's point. On August 1st, it set a new crest record of 49.47 feet at St. Louis. In total, 92 locations set record crests during the Great Flood of 1993. After it was all over, some 50,000 homes were destroyed, or damaged, with 75 towns completely inundated. The final price tag in dollars would hit $15 billion, making it one of the most expensive natural disasters in U.S. history.[22][23]

* * * * * * *

The Middle East peace accords established a framework that would eventually result in the withdrawal of Israeli forces from the Gaza Strip and parts of the West Bank, and the Palestinian right to self-government within those areas through the creation of the Palestinian Authority. This status was planned to last for five years during which a permanent solution would be negotiated, with such thorny issues as the division of Jerusalem, refugees' right of return, settlements, security, and borders to be worked out later. In October 1994, Arafat, Rabin, and Peres would be jointly awarded the Nobel Peace Prize for their efforts at reconciliation.[24] Then, in September 1995, Rabin, Arafat and Peres signed another agreement that provided for the expansion of Palestinian self-rule in the West Bank, Judea and Samaria, and for democratic elections to determine the leadership of the Palestinian Authority. The framework for this agreement had also been negotiated between April 1993 and August 20, 1993.

However, the Peace Accords were not without serious opposition, both within Israel, and inside the Palestinian community. Within Israel, Likud Party leaders Ariel Sharon and Benjamin Netanyahu indicated that should they come to power they would not honor the agreement. Jewish settlers, on the other hand, warned of violent resistance to the removal of any settlements. With each new terrorist attack against Israel in the months following the accord, attacks that were supposed to end, anxiety mounted against the agreement. The attacks were mostly coming from the Palestinian group Hamas, with its radical approach gaining in popularity after the signing of the accords, which were viewed by many Palestinians as a sell-out by Arafat. Then, in November 1995, an assassin would kill Rabin, architect of the "land for peace" effort.[25]

★ ★ ★ ★ ★ ★ ★

With the best of intentions, U. S. Middle East policy had become one of bartering the "Promised Land" in return for a promised peace. As Israel's best friend in the world, and the only superpower, the U.S. was in a unique position to pressure the Jews into concessions, and did so. The fruit of those efforts, and secret negotiations from April to August 1993, resulted in a peace accord whose ultimate goal was the removal of the ancient lands of Judea and Samaria from Israel. Unwittingly, U.S. Middle East policy had again challenged a direct promise of God, according to the ancient writings. Alongside that challenge, however, what was described as "one of the most significant and damaging natural disasters ever to hit the United States" unfolded from April to August, month-by-month, with negotiations that led to the accord. [26]

CHAPTER SEVEN

The Northridge Earthquake

I n the 1967 Six-Day War, Israel captured the areas known Biblically as Samaria and Judea from the nation of Jordan. Within Judea stood the Holy city of Jerusalem and, along with it, a history of great significance to the Jews. Jordan, like Syria and Egypt, had been poised to strike Israel with what they hoped would be a knockout blow to the very existence of the Jewish state. But Israel, aware of the impending strike, hit first, defeating the combined Arab armies. After routing the army that had intended to "drive the Jews into the sea,"[1] Israel captured the entire Sinai Desert from Egypt. However, except for a tiny area, the land within the Sinai Desert was not part of the ancient "Promised Land" in Hebrew Scriptures, according to Ezekiel.

Sinai was ultimately returned to Egypt in the peace agreement engineered by former President Jimmy Carter. Syria, on the other hand, had lost a militarily strategic area called the Golan Heights. Before the Six-Day War, the Syrian army would use this area to fire artillery shells into Israeli towns and villages within range. The military advantage afforded by the area was clear. As a plateau overlooking the Israeli side of the border, it allowed Syrian artillery marksmen to take aim at the targets below. And much to the dismay of the Israeli citizens who lived there, this advantage was used all too often.[2]

In the ancient Hebrew Scriptures, the area of the Golan Heights was included as lands promised to the Jews by God. The Israeli tribes of Dan and Manasseh occupied the region, known in ancient times as Basham.[3] As a part of ancient Jewish lands now recovered in the Six-Day War, Israel annexed the Golan Heights in 1981, adding its land to Israel proper. Religious Jews believed that this ancient land of Canaan had always belonged to Israel, although the claim was not recognized by international law.

In 1973, Syria and Egypt would launch another Middle East war in an attempt to take back the lands lost in 1967. Initially, both Arab armies made significant gains in that war, having caught the Israeli Defense Forces unprepared. Egypt drove deep into the Sinai Desert within the first several days of the war, while Syria accomplished the same in the Golan Heights. The attacks were timed to coincide with the Jewish Holy time called Yom Kippur, a major holiday when many Israeli military personnel were away from their units and celebrating with their families. But Israel was quick to regroup, and would ultimately come back in that war to once again defeat both Arab armies, as well as threatening both the Syria and Egyptian capitals.[4] After the Yom Kippur War, all of the lands captured in the 1967 Six-Day War, the Golan Heights, the West Bank, and the Sinai Desert, remained in Israel's possession.

The Jordanian Government would ultimately relinquish the West Bank (Samaria and Judea) to the Palestinians allowing them to grapple over it with the Israelis, with that dispute continuing to this day. The Sinai Desert would later be returned to Egypt in 1979. With a solution found for both Egypt and Jordan, Syria then became odd-man-out among the three combatants, as Israel continued to control the Golan Heights.

The loss of the Golan Heights was bitter for the Syrians, even though they had used it to launch wars of aggression against the Jews. As a military dictatorship, Syria, led by Hafez al-Assad, relied heavily on its relationship with the Soviet Union to supply its military with modern arms and spare parts. Much of the assistance came in the form of direct grants of aid.[5] This essentially established Syria as a client state of the "Evil Empire,"[6] as President Reagan referred to the Soviets in the 1980s. Adding to Syria's problems, its fingerprints appeared near numerous acts of terrorism, and it was not considered friendly to the United States.

After the fall of the Soviet Union in 1994, the new government of Russia expressed a willingness to work with, and not against the United States to foster peace in the region.[7] With this development, Syria lost its main source for sophisticated weapons systems. It attempted to recover from this loss by establishing new military relationships, and arms purchases from China, and North Korea. But without a superpower to back it, Syria's position in the region was weakened. As a result Syria began making overtures that "peace" with Israel was now possible.[8]

This foreign policy change coming from Damascus generated some hope within the Clinton Administration that perhaps the time was right to seek a peace agreement between the two countries. With the prodding of his Secretary of State, Warren Christopher, Clinton agreed to meet with the Syrian leader Assad in Geneva, Switzerland on January 16, 1994.[9]

The purpose of the meeting was to discuss the Middle East peace process. In a five-hour meeting, the Syrian leader openly stated to President Clinton that he was ready to establish normal relations with Israel, in exchange for the Syrian lands captured in the 1967 Six-Day War. Assad said "If the leaders of Israel have sufficient courage to respond, a new era of security and stability in which there are normal peaceful relations among all shall dawn."

Then, only two days after the Clinton-Assad meeting, Israeli Prime Minister Yitzhak Rabin issued a statement warning his fellow Israelis that they should be ready to pay "a painful price" for peace with Syria.[10] The "painful price" he was alluding to was a return of the Golan Heights to their old adversary. But although Rabin was dedicated to trading the land for what he believed would be peace, he proposed, much to the Syrians' displeasure, that the idea should be decided by a national referendum. Syria, one of the world's most oppressive dictatorships, realized that the voters of Israel were much less susceptible to pressure from President Clinton than the Israeli leadership, and found the idea absurd. They were, no doubt, correct. Voters could remember the artillery attacks initiated against Israeli towns from the Golan Heights prior to the Six-Day War.

The announcement by Prime Minister Rabin came on January 18, only two days after the Clinton-Assad meeting. This was probably a result of pressure from President Clinton. Clinton had decided to commit his powerful office to the goal of removing lands from Israel that were clearly a part of the "Promised Land" given to the Jews in the ancient texts.

THE NORTHRIDGE EARTHQUAKE

On January 17, 1994, within 24 hours of the Clinton-Assad meeting, the second most destructive natural disaster in the history of the United States struck at 4:30 A.M., Pacific Standard Time. A severe earthquake, registering 6.7 on the Richter scale, hit the San Fernando Valley 20 miles northwest of downtown Los Angeles, about one mile south-southwest of Northridge, California. The Northridge Earthquake, as it would be called, caused massive damage, killing 57 people and injuring over 9000 more. Second only at that time to Hurricane Andrew in terms of financial damage, some estimates of the total cost associated with the quake would exceed $25 billion. The Northridge Earthquake was the highest instrumentally recorded earthquake in an urban area in North American history. Although the quake occurred near the famous San Andreas Fault, it was actually caused by a fault line that was previously undiscovered. Such a fault line is described as a blind-thrust-fault.[11][12][13]

In the Book of Ezekiel in chapter 37, "The Valley of Dry Bones", the prophet records the words of God concerning Israel coming back into the "Promised Land".

Then he said unto me, Son of man, these bones are the whole house of Israel: behold, they say, Our bones are dried, and our hope is lost: we are cut off for our parts. Therefore prophesy and say unto them, Thus saith the Lord GOD; Behold, O my people, I will open your graves, and cause you to come up out of your graves, and bring you into the land of Israel

Perhaps, it was just another coincidence, but another historically severe "coincidence" that struck just as the Jews were being pressed to act against the promise from God. Coincidences do happen. But at some point, as coincidences mount, they should become suspect. Ezekiel points out the hopelessness of any possibility of the nation of Israel coming back into existence, after having been placed in *graves* for over 2000 years. The nation of Israel had about as much chance of coming back into existence as dried old bones coming back to life. Certainly, any reasonable person would have agreed that it was hard to imagine so ancient a nation coming back into existence in the twentieth century. In comparison, imagine the Aztec Empire coming back into existence next year? It isn't easy. Yet even though the ancient Jewish people were dispersed *among the heathen* more than 1500 years before the Aztecs disappeared, they came back, just as God told Ezekiel. Interestingly, the story of "The Valley of Dry Bones" notes that the return of Israel will come in stages. Consider the ancient texts:

...and the bones came together, bone to his bone. And when I beheld, lo, the sinews and the flesh came up upon them, and the skin covered them above: but there was no breath in them.[14]

We know that in the beginning of the twentieth century Jews from around the world began to congregate in the region called Palestine. Perhaps that was the coming together of the bones as described in the above

69

passage. But they still had no national life in them until November 1947 when the United Nations voted to approve the Jews' absolute right to a homeland in the British protectorate, Palestine. The Jews were historically from this region of the Middle East, and this was where Ezekiel prophesized they would return. That U.N. Resolution, along with the declaration of an independent state on May 15, 1948, could very well represent the breath of life entering the reassembled body of the old, dried bones.

Once again, as a nation became involved in trying to reverse the prophecy of Ezekiel, an "act of God" of historical significance distinguished itself with timing curiously associated with the attempt. We know that the Clinton-Assad meeting took place on January 16, 1994, and we know Israeli Prime Minister Rabin suddenly came out with a statement preparing the Israeli public for the surrender of land to Syria two days later, on January 18.

As close allies it is reasonable to assume that the United States communicated to Israel the details of the meeting with Assad, probably the day after it took place. It also appears reasonable that the U.S. exercised its influence over Israel, and its agreeable Prime Minister to accept the "land for peace" proposal from Assad. The very next day, January 18, the Prime Minister, issued his statement of warning to the Israeli public concerning the Golan Heights. So it is not unreasonable to believe that pressure on Israel to give back the "Promised Land" of the Golan Heights took place sometime on January 17, 1994, the same day as the historical Northridge earthquake.

✴ ✴ ✴ ✴ ✴ ✴ ✴

Three years earlier the launching of "Madrid" coincided with the "Perfect Storm," a once in a hundred year "freak of nature" that swallowed the President's home with a 30-foot wave as he attended the opening day ceremonies. The Madrid process would soon become meaningless, stalling under the leadership of Shamir, who did not believe that trading land would buy true peace. But, everything would suddenly change with the elevation of Rabin, making the next conference in Washington, D.C. a true "land for peace" gathering, much to the delight of the Bush Administration. That joy, however, would be spoiled as the President's attention was divided between the conference and Hurricane Andrew, one of the most powerful storms ever that had just destroyed South Florida.

The conference would prove to be the catalyst of a new process, one that would ultimately result in secret negotiations between the Israelis and Palestinians, and in reducing Israeli control over the lands promised in the ancient texts. However, unfolding month-by-month along-side the negotiations would be a multi-state flood described as the "worst natural disaster in American history."

The breakthrough, signed on the White House lawn, would mark the beginning of a process between the Jews and Palestinians that would continue to unfold over the next two years. The Clinton Administration, seeking to add to that "success," would expand its drive to remove more lands in talks with Syria's Assad. The accommodating Assad would agree with Clinton, causing Rabin to announce his intention to withdraw from the Golan Heights. That announcement came the day after the second most destructive natural disaster in U.S. history struck, the Northridge Earthquake.

Perhaps these events are explainable as mere coincidence. That is for the reader to decide. But, in the years ahead, more coincidences would occur during the term of the next U.S. President, George W. Bush, with his Presidency being dramatically impacted.[15]

CHAPTER EIGHT

The Great Texas Flood

The assassin's bullet that tragically ended the life of Prime Minister Rabin would usher in a series of Israeli governments, which continued, more or less, the work that he, Arafat, and Clinton began in September 1993. During the months of negotiations leading up to the historical agreement, "one of the most significant and damaging natural disasters ever to hit the United States" unfolded month-by-month with it. The Clinton Administration, encouraged by the success of that agreement, would continue its efforts at another breakthrough in the years ahead, but to no avail.

Part of the reason for the lack of progress would rest with the Palestinian leader, Arafat, whose mouth would become an enemy equal to any against his cause. Sometimes the words of a man will get away from him, speaking what is in the heart, but not wisely. In reference to the solemn and historical agreement he had signed a year earlier, Arafat was quoted on May 10, as saying:

> This agreement, I am not considering it more than the agreement which had been signed between our prophet Muham-

mad and Quraish, and you remember that the Caliph Omar had refused this agreement and considered it a despicable truce...But the same way Muhammad had accepted it, we are now accepting this peace effort.[1]

To the American media his words had little meaning. But to Israelis, knowledgeable in the ways of Islam, its meaning was clear. Like Muhammad's truce with the unfortunate Quraish, the Palestinians intended to use the "breakthrough agreement" to ultimately destroy their partner in peace.

Perhaps Arafat was simply too proud of his duplicity, the forces of restraint within overwhelmed by exploding desires, unable to be restrained even in the most delicate of settings. Arafat would express more Palestinian goals, clear enough that any Middle East observer could understand. Speaking to diplomats in Stockholm, Sweden:

I have no use for Jews; they are and remain Jews! We now need all the help we can get from you in our battle for a united Palestine under total Arab-Muslim domination.[2]

As successive polling within the Palestinian-dominated areas had indicated, the very existence of Israel was an affront unacceptable to the majority. Since Palestinians wanted Israel to be replaced by an Arab-Muslim nation, Arafat's words were only voicing the hopes and aspirations of the people he represented, words distinctly different from those designed for the western media[3][4][5] As the Clinton years came to an end, its latest emissary was frustrated by the inability to secure another breakthrough for the troubled region. The Mitchell Committee's final report would soon be on the desk of the new President, George W. Bush, by May 2001.

Former United States Senator George Mitchell and the five members of the "fact-finding" committee arrived in Israel on December 11, 2000. The committee goal was to establish the causes of the Palestinian-Israeli dispute and make recommendations for a solution. It would spend the better part of the next five months in the region groping for an answer. The group included Mitchell, European Union foreign policy chief Javier Solana, former U.S. Senator Warren Rudman, former Turkish President Demirel, and Norwegian Foreign Minister Thorbjorn Jagland. The Mitchell Commission, as the group came to be known, would meet in the resort town of Sharm El-Sheikh in Egypt and produce what would be called the "Mitchell Report."[6]

The committee report came under immediate criticism after its release in April 2001. The primary complaint from critics was that the "fact-finding" committee had actually ignored the facts and, instead, sought the appearance of being "even handed" in the dispute. The effort to appear "even-handed" manifested itself with statements that appeared to equate terrorist killings committed by the Palestinians with the efforts Israel made to control areas where Palestinians were the dominant population. In a sarcastic reply to the Mitchell report, Daniel Pipes of the *Washington Times* observed that the commission, by refusing to judge right and wrong in the conflict, missed the mark. He then, sarcastically, went on to apply some comparisons to previous historical disputes.

> Had the Mitchell committee been asked to assess the outbreak of World War II, it would likely have regretted Hitler's crossing the Polish border, but balanced this with tsk-tsking about provocative statements coming from Warsaw. Assigned the same job for the Japanese attack on Pearl Harbor, it would have evenhandedly blamed both parties.[7]

Accusations and depictions such as these, though denied by former Senators Mitchell and Rudman, did appear to have credibility. The report appears to make excuses for the terrorist activities associated with the Palestinian cause. But among the several measures proposed by the Mitchell Report, one drew the special attention of the Israeli side. It recommended that Israel "should freeze all settlement activity, including the natural growth of existing settlements." This recommendation placed the Mitchell Committee squarely on a collision course with the ancient Hebrew Scriptures promising this land to the Jews.

Israelis viewed the measure as a Mitchell Committee gift to Yasser Arafat, a concession never negotiated in any form between the Israelis and Palestinians. Though this new requirement was placed on the Israeli side, the essential requirement of Yasser Arafat remained what it had always been, to "renounce the use of terrorism and other acts of violence." Arafat, who had promised to do that on numerous occasions over the years, thus far was unable, or unwilling, to accomplish it.

THE NEW BUSH ADMINISTRATION

At the beginning of the new Bush Presidency in early 2001, there appeared to be a concerted effort not to become too involved in the Middle East conflict. The new administration seemed to be guided by the belief that unless there was a solid reason to believe that progress could be made, diplomatic efforts on the part of the United States should be withheld. In a sense, it appeared that Bush did not want the United States to be seen failing, as so many other administrations had done when it came to the Middle East.

But, then, on June 5, 2001, the President suddenly decided to test the waters of the Middle East. Bush announced he would send CIA Director George Tenet to the region to meet with the Israelis and Palestinians in an attempt to get the recommendations of the Mitchell Report back on track.[8] The reason for this abrupt change, as reported by the *New York Times*, was that a truce between the parties had held for three days. Three days without fighting may not appear to be a very long time, but in the Middle East conflict between the Israelis and Palestinians, it was a major achievement. On June 5, the new Bush Administration held a press conference where it announced the decision to become more engaged. The ultimate goal of the process was placing restrictions on the "Promised Land" of Israel.[9]

TENET'S EFFORT

Tenet had experienced the frustrating cauldron of trouble called the Middle East during the Clinton Administration years. As CIA Director, Clinton had first used his services in an effort to build trust between Israeli and Palestinian security forces, hoping to bring some form of stability to the conflict. But, in the beginning of the Bush Administration, Tenet's role was eliminated in line with its initial hands-off policy. Now, the CIA Director was asked to go back to his former role of mediator between the two sides, but under circumstances that were even more difficult than during the Clinton years.[10][11]

Speculation mounted as to what prompted the administration to change its Middle East policy to one of greater involvement. Besides the three-day cease fire, the reason most often given was the concern that the situation could spiral out of control if there were any more serious attacks against Israel. Just the previous Friday, a suicide bomber stunned and grieved the nation by killing 20 young Israelis. One more similar attack could cause an Israeli response that would push the conflict over the brink and into regional warfare.[12]

But there could have been another motive. The German foreign minister and a United Nations official had been inside Israel for several days, and it appeared that their efforts were the reason Arafat agreed to the ceasefire. Perhaps this small "success," so rare in that part of the world, caused some concerns within the Bush Administration that the U.S. role might be eclipsed. But whatever the reason, the Bush Presidency was beginning a process that sought to remove the "Promised Land" from Israel. The presidency of George W. Bush was now on a collision course with the ancient scriptures and the prophecy of the rebirth of Israel in the "Promised Land."

THE TEXAS GREAT FLOOD

On June 5, 2001, as the White House was announcing that it was sending CIA Director George Tenet to the Middle East, weathermen in the President's home state of Texas were watching the Gulf of Mexico. That morning, just before the White House announcement, an upper-level, low-pressure system was centered 150 miles offshore in the north-western Gulf. The system "wasn't given much of a chance of strengthening," according to the *Houston Chronicle*.[13] At the National Weather Service, forecasters believed that the necessary factors for the development of a tropical storm, light high-altitude winds and a warm sea surface, were missing. But by 2 P. M. on June 5, just after the White House announcement, an Air Force reserve Hurricane Hunter aircraft flew into the weather system and discovered it was suddenly a full-blown tropical storm, just off the coast of Texas! The core temperatures were warmer than expected, causing the winds to intensify quickly during the day.[14] According to an official at the National Weather Service, "The storm developed so rapidly, there was no time to react."[15]

The mystery storm caught the National Weather service off guard. The Center's seven computer models had all predicted a different outcome from what had just developed.[16] Charles Roeseler, a forecaster at the National Weather Service, observed "It went right from nothing to a tropical storm!"[17] According to the *Houston Chronicle*, "The storm had not even been a blip on the forecaster's radar screens twelve hours earlier, before it became the first named storm of the hurricane season." All of this took place on June 5th.[18]

Typically, a tropical storm will develop somewhere between Africa and the Caribbean, leaving the residents of Texas with days to consider the need to buy provisions, board up windows, or to evacuate. But because this storm had instantly developed just off of the coast, the residents of the President's home state literally had no time to react. The storm moved slowly bringing massive bands of showers, causing the Texas counties of Harris, Brazoria, and Galveston to be soaked. The rainfall from the lingering storm would eventually deposit a near record amount, and bringing with it massive flooding.

Tropical Storm Allison would turn into what meteorologists consider to be the "nation's worst tropical storm" ever and unanimously "decreed by weather experts as a deluge of historic proportions for its rainfall totals, flooding and widespread effect."[19] Quite a distinction for a weather system that was not even considered a storm on the morning of June 5, but by that afternoon was a named tropical storm just off the coast, its impact severely felt by that evening. Allison left a lasting mark on the Houston area, including 22 deaths, 70,000 homes damaged, and over $5 billion in area damage. At the College of Medicine in Baylor, countless research projects were delayed or destroyed when over 30,000 lab animals drowned.[20]

Part of the reason for the massive damage from Allison was that it did what very few storms in history have ever done. After suddenly developing on June 5, and striking the Houston area with no warning, it moved on only to come back and attack again on the evening of June 8, dumping an extraordinary amount of rain on the area. Some parts of Houston received an amazing 36 inches over several days. Some areas received over 25 inches of rain in a 24-hour period! That 24-hour total was only exceeded once in Texas history by a tropical storm.[21]

There were images of severe flooding in downtown Houston, comparable only to those of New Orleans, four years later, caused by Hurricane Katrina. Because of its unusually destructive nature, the World Meteorological Organization Regional Association decided to retire the name Allison as an Atlantic storm name. For a storm name to be retired, it must have caused a great degree of damage and have been a storm of historical proportions.

CONCLUSION

Once again an unusually powerful and damaging act of God appeared on the scene just at the exact time an American president became involved in the Middle East "peace" process, where the goal was to remove land promised to Israel in ancient Hebrew Scriptures. In this case it was the effort to revive the Mitchell Committee's report as a basis for "peace" in the conflict. Although the intentions of the administration were noble, sending a presidential representative to the area for this purpose placed the United States in the corner of restricting the use of the land that was "promised" long ago to the Jews. This land was inhabited in ancient times by the Jews as part of the nations of Israel and Judea, before their foretold scattering among the nations. Now back in the Jew's possession, have these lands become a great stumbling block to the nations of the world? With the "Great Flood of 2001," as it was christened by the *Houston Chronicle*, we have another example of an unusual natural phenomena taking place, "coincidental," to an effort to remove the "Promised Land" from the Jews. However, later in that same fateful year 2001, another coincidence of much greater magnitude would occur, with timing once again related to the ancient lands promised in those very old writings.[22]

CHAPTER NINE

September 11, 2001

I t was the worst moment in the complicated relationship between the United States and oil rich Saudi Arabia. The Saudis had just joined the oil embargo against the U.S. after President Nixon initiated a massive military resupply of the Israelis during the Yom Kippur War. The year was 1973; Egypt and Syria had launched a coordinated surprise attack against Israel in an effort to secure the lands they lost in the 1967 Six-Day War and, hopefully, "drive her into the sea." This war, and the oil embargo that followed, would mark a critical turning point in the relationship between Saudi Arabia and the United States. From that point forward, the relationship started by Franklin Roosevelt, and nurtured by presidents since, would find the U.S. needing to deal with the desert kingdom with much greater care.[1] At the time of the Yom Kippur War, the United States was importing about 25% of its oil to keep the wheels of industry and its vehicles moving. Saudi Arabia, the biggest oil exporter in the world, was the main source. As a result of the embargo, the price of crude oil went from $3 a barrel to a staggering $11 in less than a month, causing serious economic issues in the western economies. Oil prices would remain at that level and climb even higher in the years ahead, resulting in a massive shift in wealth from oil consuming nations to oil-producing ones.[2]

The embargo took the United States by surprise. Ever since the mutually beneficial relationship of oil for security began in the 1940s, the Saudis had been a reliable ally in the cauldron of trouble called the Middle East. But in 1973, Saudi leadership, headed by King Faisal, responded to pressure from fellow Arabs, and acquiesced by joining the embargo. As the home of Islam's top holy city, Mecca, the Saudis were viewed as having a special responsibility in the eyes of conservative Muslims across the world. That responsibility was watched over by the Whahabi clerics within the kingdom who exercised much influence in matters relating to Islam. These clerics pressed the king to use the oil weapon against the United States for its support of Israel, and they were heard.[3]

The relationship would eventually be pieced back together in the ensuing months. Neither nation could truly afford a permanent break. All would be well between the two until August 2001. But unlike the strain in 1973, the 2001 crisis would approach the point of a break, something unimaginable to the U.S. government.

* * * * * *

As the suicide bomber aimed his deadly cargo at its target, he could see the American Embassy straight ahead. The Americans securing the complex in Nairobi, Kenya, were caught off guard. The building was vulnerable. The explosive-laden truck would be there in just a moment, and its driver, Muhammad Rashed Daoud al-Owhali, would soon be dead, his mission completed. But, unlike the driver of the second truck-bomb striking another target simultaneously in Tanzania, Owhali began having second thoughts about departing this world. The promised virgins of the afterlife would have to wait for another day.

With just enough time to avoid the blast he would soon be the cause of, Owhali swung open the door to the truck. He flew out, escaping in the mayhem that followed. He would take refuge in one of Nairobi's cheap hotels, waiting to be smuggled out of the country by his compatriots. However, in that summer of 1998, the FBI would find him first, getting a badly needed break, with Owhali becoming an invaluable source of information. He led them to wiretap a previously unknown al-Qaeda "safe house" in Yemen. Those wire taps would reveal information about an al-Qaeda summit to be held in Malaysia in January 2000.[4, 5]

★ ★ ★ ★ ★ ★ ★

After the administration of George W. Bush took power in January 2001, the new president quickly gained a reputation in Saudi Arabia, and other Middle Eastern nations, as a lightweight on the peace process between Israel and the Palestinians. In a three-part series of articles in February 2002, *Washington Post* staff writers Robert Kaiser and David Ottaway took an in-depth look into relations between the two countries in the days just prior to September 11th. They reported that on August 9, 2001, the Saudi Ambassador to Britain, Ghazi Qussaibi, was quoted in a London-based Arabic newspaper as saying that Bush knows very little, and is ruled by "complexes," the most important, to avoid looking like his predecessor and his father. Qussaibi went on to say that the President had already accomplished making enemies out of friends for America in the short time he had been in the White House. The main issue of contention appeared to be centered on the Palestinian-Israeli conflict. To the dismay of the Saudi kingdom, including its leader Crown Prince Abdullah, George Bush seemed to have a very simple policy, whatever Israeli leader Sharon wanted, he got.[6, 7]

In fact, Bush was quite supportive of the Israeli leaders' position, which essentially was that, before any real progress could be made toward peace, the Palestinians would have to end terror attacks against

Israel. In line with that view, he refused to restrain Israel from taking actions against the Palestinians to prevent further terrorist actions. But, to the Muslim world, this represented giving Israel a blank check. From the Arabs' perspective, President Bush was not following the "balanced approach" of the Clinton Administration. Certainly, with the new Bush administration's hands off policy clear to all, there was no indication that the president would be amenable to the establishment of a Palestinian state, which no American president had ever supported. Therefore, President Bush was not pushing for a division of the lands promised the Jews in the Hebrew Scriptures, at least not yet. Under these conditions, the Saudi-American relationship, critical to both nations, was now ripe for a very wide break, and one soon came.

Sensing trouble and desiring to head it off, the Bush administration tried several times to calm Abdullah. The efforts included a personal invitation from Bush to visit Camp David, the Bush ranch in Crawford, Texas, as well as Washington. The elder Bush even telephoned Abdullah to put in a good word for the younger Bush, indicating that his sons "heart was in the right place."[8] But none of the efforts appeared to have any impact. The anger persisted on the part of the Saudis.[9][10]

As an Islamic monarchy ruled by the Saud family, in close cooperation with Islamic fundamentalists, the Saudis found the U.S. policy of strong support for Israel very disturbing. This was the same Saudi Arabia that possessed an environment from which came 15 of the 19 hijackers associated with the September 11, 2001 terrorist attacks, causing many in the west to ask how an "ally" of the United States could produce most of the individuals that sacrificed their lives in order to hurt America. The answer to that question can only be found within the dichotomy of conflicting faces that is Saudi Arabia.

As an Islamic fundamentalist nation with a small population, but enormous natural wealth, in a neighborhood with nations that have very large populations, but much less wealth, therein lies the dilemma. Saudi Arabia needs protection from those around it otherwise one of the Persian Gulf nations, like Iran or Iraq, would quickly gobble it up, taking with it the better part of the world's oil reserves and incredible wealth. If the world is an oyster, Saudi Arabia is its pearl of oil. This understanding is not lost upon the minds of the ruling Saud family. Therefore, Saudi Arabia has both the need, and the willingness, to "guarantee" reasonably-priced, stable, and reliable oil in exchange for "guarantees" of security from the United States. Yet the very act of engaging the United States for this security tends to strengthen internal and external Islamic opponents of the royal family and, thus, creates a different kind of security problem for the Kingdom. As a result, occasionally, the Saudis need to defy the United States in the name of Islam. So it was in 1973, during the Yom Kippur war, and again in August 2001, as the Palestinian Intifada against Israel increasingly agitated the situation in the Middle East.

The Intifada was a massive Palestinian uprising against Israeli rule ranging from civil disobedience to violence, and including general strikes and boycotts. Since the nightly news usually showed the image of a rock-throwing Palestinian youth against an Israeli tank or armored vehicle, the international attention was almost entirely negative for the Israelis. These images, broadcast around the globe, helped produce the developing rift in relations between the desert kingdom of Saudi Arabia and Israel's main backer, the militarily powerful United States. The arranged marriage of sorts between these two completely different cultures had finally hit what appeared to be an insurmountable obstacle.[11]

* * * * * * *

The CIA operatives were very quiet, their mission, very secretive. They had tracked their prey, Khaled al-Mihdhar, to a hotel in Dubai, a stopover on his way to the al-Qaeda summit in Malaysia. There he would meet with his brothers, not of blood, but in hatred against America. Inside the hotel room, leaving no sign of entry, the CIA agents would find what they were looking for. Not long after, the photographs of Mihdhar's passport would be in the hands of CIA officials halfway across the world.

For the Malaysia summit, the CIA would have the help of that government's intelligence community, the "Special Branch" as it was called. They placed the January 5, 2000 meeting Mihdhar was to attend under surveillance. That effort would net photographs of a dozen or so al-Qaeda members present with their leader, Osama bin Laden, but in a stunning oversight, the meeting was not bugged for eavesdropping. Had it been, plans for 9/11, as well as the bombing of the USS Cole, might have been discovered.

There were other signs that the CIA was slipping. On January 8, three days after the summit, Special Branch would notify them that Mihdhar and two other al-Qaeda members that had attended were leaving together. Their destination was Bangkok, Thailand. One of the men, Khallad, would meet with the men that would later bomb the USS Cole. Then, several months later, the CIA would observe the third man, Hani, entering the United States with none other than Mihdhar. Now, some of the dots of a potential terrorist conspiracy, developing within the United States, were beginning to come together as bin Laden associates made their way into the country. Standard CIA procedure dictated notifying the FBI, State Department, and INS of their presence since its mandate ended at America's shore. Notifying these agencies would allow them to track, or arrest, the terrorists within the United States. Tragically, the CIA would fail to share this information with its sister agencies until just before September 2001.[12][13]

THE SAUDI-AMERICAN BREAK

In the *Washington Post* article, Kaiser and Ottaway indicated that a little less than three weeks before the September 11 attacks, Saudi Crown

Prince Abdullah watched President Bush's live news conference from Crawford, Texas. The Crown Prince had recently witnessed an Israeli soldier place his boot on the face of an elderly Palestinian woman. With that image fresh in his mind, the Prince heard Bush complain that the Palestinians had again undermined the peace process with more violence. Bush went on to explain that for the peace process to move forward, "Mr. Arafat [must] put 100% effort into ...stopping the terrorist activity." He further stated that "...the Israelis will not negotiate under terror threat. Simple as that!"[14]

That was all that Prince Abdullah could handle. According to the article, Abdullah "just went bananas" after listening to Bush's remarks at the news conference. The Prince interpreted the President's remarks as placing all of the blame for the lack of progress on Mr. Arafat and the Palestinians, absolving the Israelis of any blame whatsoever.[15]

The Prince called his ambassador to the United States, Prince Bandar Bin Sultan. Bandar, the son of Saudi defense minister Prince Sultan, was a long time fixture of the diplomatic community in Washington. When Abdullah reached him, he found out that Bandar had watched the same news conference. At his palatial residence in Aspen, Colorado, Bandar received instructions from Abdullah to deliver a very harsh and threatening letter to President Bush. He was instructed to personally deliver the letter from Abdullah directly to the President.

In his book, "State of Denial," Bob Woodward described the scene as Bandar delivered the message. According to Woodward, Bandar began:

> Mr. President, this is the most difficult message I have had to convey to you that I have ever conveyed between the two governments since I started working here in Washington in 1982. Mr. President, leadership in Saudi Arabia always has to feel the pulse of the people and then reflect the feelings of the people in its policies.[16][17]

According to Woodward's book, Bandar went on to applaud the President's father, whose administration had cancelled loan guarantees to the Israelis after they violated their promise on settlements and who was viewed as having a "balanced policy" in the conflict. But then he added that the "Crown Prince has tried to find many excuses for this administration and we couldn't."[18]

According to Woodward's book, as well as the Kaiser and Ottaway series of articles, it was reported that the letter stated the Saudi government understood "there has been a strategic decision by the United States that its national interest in the Middle East is 100% based on [Israeli Prime Minister] Sharon." This, the letter went on, "is America's right, but that Saudi Arabia could not accept it." Then the leader of Saudi Arabia stated something that represented a threat, unprecedented in the long relationship between the two countries. He indicated that the United States could go its way in the Middle East, and Saudi Arabia would go its way. Saudi Arabia would no longer look out for the interests of the U.S. in the region, but only for its own interests, regardless of what the interests of the U.S. might be.

Within the emotional letter from Abdullah were depictions of how he saw the belief system that guided U.S. policy toward the Palestinians. He stated, "I reject this extraordinary, un-American bias whereby the blood of an Israeli child is more expensive and holy than the blood of a Palestinian child. I reject people that say when you kill a Palestinian it is self defense; when a Palestinian kills an Israeli, a terrorist act." He went on to write about the scene of the Israeli soldier with his boot on the face of the Palestinian woman. Sensing that a break of potentially historic proportions was at hand, the Bush Administration looked to act immediately to address the crisis.[19][20]

The Kaiser-Ottoway article indicated that after delivering the message, Bandar was told to inform Bush that his next instructions from his government were to completely break off all contact between the two countries, as it was time to "get busy rearranging our lives in the Middle East." In line with that new Saudi approach to relations, things began to change immediately. On August 24, Saudi Chief of Staff General Muhayya arrived in Washington for a high level review of Saudi-U.S. military relations. But on the 25th, he spoke to Bandar by telephone and was informed that Abdullah was ordering him to leave immediately, and return home without meeting any American military officials. In Saudi Arabia, 40 military officers were ordered to disembark a plane they had just boarded which was to take them to the United States for the military meeting. The meeting with U.S. military officials was cancelled.

The Abdullah letter sent shock waves through the Bush White House. Stunned officials within the new administration scrambled to find an answer, one that would begin the process of healing. A break with Saudi Arabia in the Middle East, from which the United States was now receiving over half of its oil in 2001, would impair the U.S. ability to deal with a multitude of issues critical to the economic and national security interest of the country. The administration needed to act dramatically to address the break. It did very quickly and in a way that would surprise Saudi Arabia.[21][22]

* * * * * * *

Shortly after the al-Qaeda summit, more ripe intelligence fruit would be available for the CIA to pick. Leaving the terrorist meeting, two al-Qaeda operatives, Nawaf Alhazmi and Khalid Almihdar would both board a plane headed for Los Angeles. Having entered the United States, they became easy prey for arrest, or better yet, they could be followed to uncover their mission. Often, tracking such individuals within the U.S. leads to others within the country that are involved in planning a terrorist attack—and can result in a major break for the United States internal security. But for 21 months the CIA would fail to alert the domestic U.S. agencies. During that time Alhazmi and Almihdar would move about the country freely, obtaining drivers licenses and opening bank accounts. More ominously, they would both enroll in flight school. Had the CIA notified the proper domestic agencies concerning the presence of these two within the U.S., they would have been simple to capture or track to discover their mission. Instead, when Almihdar's visa expired in June, 2001, he would simply walk into a State Department office and receive a new one just for asking. Because his name had not been placed on the ter-rorist watch list, the Department was free to reissue the visa. Yet, by the time he walked into the State Department, the CIA could link him not only to the al-Qaeda summit, but also to the USS Cole bombers as well.

Later, before the Senate Committee investigating 9/11, the CIA would take the position that Alhazmi and Almihdar had not yet been identified as potential terrorists in January 2000, when they entered the United States. This conclusion was drawn, in spite of the fact that both had just left an al-Qaeda summit in Malaysia attended by bin Laden.[23][24]

THE BUSH RESPONSE

Bush's response came in the form of a letter delivered to Saudi Am-bassador Bandar only 36 hours after he received Abdullah's letter. Again, according to Kaiser and Ottaway's *Washington Post* series, the Saudis saw the letter as "groundbreaking." It gave an approach to the Arab-Israeli dispute that differed considerably from what Israeli Prime Minister Sha-ron was pursuing and pleased the Saudis greatly. Bush went on to say in his response that he rejected the humiliation of individuals and that he believed the innocent blood of a Palestinian, Israeli, Jew, Christian or Muslim is all the same. Then, what Bush said next represented one of the most dramatic reversals in U.S. official policy. The president stated:

I firmly believe the Palestinian people have a right to self-deter-
mination and to live peacefully and securely in their own state,
in their own homeland, just as the Israelis have the right to live
peacefully and safely in their own state.

The announcement that the Bush administration would now support the establishment of a Palestinian state stunned the Saudis about
as much as Prince Abdullah's letter stunned the Bush Administration.
Support for a Palestinian state by the U.S. government was a drastic departure in its approach to the conflict. According to Woodward, even the
Clinton Administration had never ventured to propose such a thing in
its eight years of Middle East diplomacy.[25][26]

The land for the new state of Palestine, now envisioned and supported by Bush, would come from the ancient lands of Judea and Samaria,
promised to the Jews in the Hebrew Scriptures, and possessed by the descendents of Ezekiel since the 1967 Six-Day War. The new Bush policy,
if realized, would remove large tracts of the "Promised Land" from Israel
on a permanent basis, completely negating the ancient promises purported to be from God to the Jews. But from the perspective of the new
administration, the Bush letter and its dramatic change in U.S. Middle
East policy appeared to have the desired impact on Abdullah, placating
him and the Saudi ruling class.

After the delivery of the letter to Abdullah, Bush's reputation within
the small circle of Saudis that rule the country went "from rock bottom
to sky high," according to Kaiser and Ottaway. Bush was no longer the
lightweight American President, but a statesman with strength and vision. Abdullah was so impressed with this groundbreaking letter he
decided to share it with the heads of other Arab nations. He even sum-
moned Arafat to Riyadh to read it personally. The same *Washington Post*
article also reported that on Friday, September 7, 2001 U.S. officials indicated an eagerness to implement the new policy immediately. This, the

Saudis observed, was a sharp departure from Bush's first seven months in office, when the administration was unwilling to become involved in the Middle East conflict unless there were clear signs that an agreement had already been worked out.

Over the weekend, on September 8 and 9, officials from both countries began planning what would happen next. The approach decided upon was to introduce the new U.S. policy to the world with a Bush speech, and possibly one from Secretary of State Powell. Both would officially call for the establishment of a Palestinian state. According to Woodard, in *State of Denial,* Bush agreed to publicly come out for a Palestinian state in a "big rollout" planned for the week of September 10, 2001.

* * * * * * *

On August 23, 2001, the CIA would finally send the much needed cable to the State Department, INS, Customs and the FBI requesting that "bin Laden-related individuals" have their names added to the terror watch list. Alhazmi and Almihdar, and several others would now be sought within U.S. borders for the first time. The late actions on the part of the CIA were partly the result of the FBI analyst assigned to the CIA's Counter Terrorism Center, Margaret Gillespie, who had pressed for the cable to be sent. Her actions motivated CIA Director George Tenet to order an urgent review of all files within the agency, resulting in the August 23 cable.[27][28]

Although the late revelation of Alhazmi and Almihdar's entry was being disseminated to powerful U.S. government agencies now, in a stunning oversight, it was not shared with the FAA and the Treasury Department's Financial Crimes Enforcement Network, neither the FBI's Financial Review Group. With the power to tap financial data, these organizations would have almost certainly found the trail of debit and credit card transactions where multiple airline tickets had been purchased by the Middle Eastern men. It is likely this would have led to the FBI meeting the plotters at the airport, arresting them before they could board their flights that would soon become weapons of mass destruction.

In spite of the late hour in which the critical information reached domestic agencies, there was yet another chance to prevent the attack that was now only days away. The State Department, now adding the names to the terrorist list that tracked international flights, in a stunning, and grievous oversight, left them off of the domestic one. The last chance to stop 9/11 had been missed.[29][30]

THE ATTACK

A violation of United States territory by a foreign enemy has been rare in the history of the republic. The first was the invasion of a very young United States by the British in the War of 1812. The second was Pearl Harbor on the "day that would live in infamy," December 7, 1941. The blessing of such rare invasions has allowed America to become the most stable and prosperous nation in world history. Because America has not been the recipient of attacks from foreign enemies with any degree of frequency, it has become a beacon of liberty, and an "arsenal of democracy" in a world that suffered two world wars in the 20th Century. But the cover of protection that kept America safe was lifted during the week of September 10, 2001.

That week the new President, George W. Bush, intended to announce a major shift in U.S. Middle East policy to the world. It would be a policy that for the first time resulted in U.S. support for a Palestinian state on a large portion of the lands that were given to the Jews by God.

Early on the morning of September 11, 2001, Alhazmi, Almihdhar and seventeen other hijackers, using box-cutter knives and chemical spray, took control of four airliners. All four airliners were destined for West Coast airports which assured that they would have the maximum fuel on board. The first to inflict its dastardly harm was American Airlines Flight 11, which crashed into the World Trade Center North Tower at 8:46 a.m., followed by United Airlines Flight 175 which hit the South Tower at 9:03 a.m. Shortly afterward, at 9:37 a.m. American Airlines Flight 77 crashed into the Pentagon. Ultimately, the forth airliner, United Airlines Flight 93 would crash in a field in Pennsylvania killing everyone on board. That plane, apparently destined for either the White House or U.S. Capital, was prevented from reaching its target by the bravery of the passengers on board. The terrorist organization Al-Qaeda was found to be responsible for the attacks which killed 3000 Americans. Like Pearl Harbor, it would mark the beginning of war for America, the War on Terrorism, which would lead to the invasion of both Afghanistan and Iraq by the United States.[31]

All of the terrorists were eventually identified by the FBI when, by pure happenstance, the luggage of their leader, Mohamed Atta, containing a trove of mission documents, did not make its connecting flight. Based on the mission documents found in his luggage, it was determined that fifteen of the nineteen hijackers were from Saudi Arabia.

In his book *Eye to Eye*, William Koenig details the degree of destruction caused by the events of September 11, 2001. He points out that the lives lost on that fateful day exceeded those lost at Pearl Harbor.[32]

CONCLUSION

The week of September 10, 2001 saw an event of historic proportions take place on United States soil, an attack that killed more Americans than the Japanese attack on Pearl Harbor in 1941. Yet that very same week, the Bush administration's new Middle East policy was to be announced. For the first time, the United States would support an independent Palestinian state on land's known in the ancient Hebrew Scriptures as Judea and Samaria. The restoration of these lands had been foretold by scripture, a prophecy that they would be restored to an Israeli nation that would come back after having been *scattered among the nations* for over 2000 years.

Since that prophetic event in 1948, all nations that attempted to take back the land suffered from their efforts. This lesson was best known to the multitude of angry Arab countries surrounding the out numbered, and out gunned Jews. Each time they met on the battlefield, regardless of the odds, the modern day Israelites would gain more of the ancient "Promised Land." Now exhausted from attempting to "drive the Jews into the sea" using their armies, her Arab enemies would use the good offices of other nations to do their bidding. As the lone superpower in the world, and especially vulnerable to the "oil weapon," the United States was called upon to do the job for them.

The change in the Bush administration's Middle East policy represented one of the sharpest policy turning points of any American president. After a hands-off attitude toward the conflict, except for the George Tenet visit announced June 5, 2001, Bush shifted all the way to calling for the establishment of a Palestinian state. No previous American President had been willing to go that far. The big rollout announcing U.S. support for a Palestinian state was set for the week of September 10, 2001.[33]

CHAPTER TEN

562 Tornados

I n 1947, the newly formed United Nations voted to partition British-
mandated Palestine into two states, one Jewish and the other Arab.
But in 1948, only one state became a reality, the Jewish one called Israel.
The problem on the Arab side was that the Palestinians, and the nations
of Jordan and Egypt, could not come together on the concept of a new
Arab state. This was because, by agreeing to the creation of a new Arab
state, the Arab nations and Palestinian Arabs would effectively be legiti-
mizing the new Jewish state as well. This, the Arab side was unwilling
to do, even if it meant the prevention of the new Arab state. But their
attempt to stop the birth of the Jewish nation would prove unsuccessful,
in spite of the incredible odds favoring Arab forces. Israel was destined to
win its war for independence, and in the end, it was the new Arab nation
that died. Having not taken advantage of the United Nations plan, but
instead focusing on preventing the Jews from realizing their dream, the
road to nationhood would become a very difficult one for the Palestinians from that time forward.[1]

However, after over 50 years of attempting to create the Arab state,
Palestine, the government of Israel, and representatives of the Palestinians

were on the verge of doing just that in the year 2000. A final agreement for the partition of land, as well as peace, was ready to be consummated. But, once again, the Palestinian side refused to legitimize the state of Israel and rejected the deal in the eleventh hour.[2] Therefore, the refusal of the Palestinian leadership to accept the existence of a Jewish state appears to be the main reason there is no Palestinian nation. Unfortunately for those seeking a peaceful solution to the conflict, the problem of establishing real peace was even more difficult than overcoming the Palestinian leadership. The problem actually rested with the perceptions and beliefs of the Palestinian people themselves.

Successive polling of the Palestinian people, conducted by both Israeli and Palestinian pollsters, revealed that a majority of Palestinians reject the legitimacy and permanence of Israel. Additionally, the majority of those polled appeared to support terrorism as well as the "right of return" to Israel, which would effectively dissolve the Jewish state. The desire to extinguish Israel, therefore, appears to be common among Palestinians. Daniel Mandel in *The Review*, a Melbourne-based foreign policy journal, states the Palestinian populace places its version of "justice" against Israel above the desire for nationhood. This ideology appears to prevent the Palestinian leadership from negotiating effectively with Israel. He writes:

> In this sense, mainstream Palestinian opinion is not moderate, and terrorism draws not upon socioeconomic frustration, but upon the wider aspirations of Palestinian nationalism.

This appears to explain why the Palestinian leadership's efforts to reign-in terrorism continues to fall short; because terrorism does not emanate from a fringe element within their society, but, rather, from its center.[3]

Against this backdrop, President George W. Bush launched his "road map" peace plan designed to create a Palestinian state. A Palestinian state whose leadership and people would, undoubtedly, be dedicated to the extinction of the Jewish state next door. The genesis of the "road map" was Saudi crown prince Abdullah's peace initiative, endorsed by the Arab League. This plan called for "normal relations" with Israel, and, in return, Israel would withdraw to the pre-Six-Day War borders and confirm a Palestinian "right of return" to Israel proper. The "right of return" aspect would have effectively ended the Jewish state by diluting it, essentially, destroying it from within. Because of this requirement, far from being true peace, the "road map" agreement would have brought the Arab dream of extinguishing the life of Israel several steps closer.

THE QUARTET'S CONFERENCE

On April 30, 2003, the Middle East Quartet formally launched the long awaited "road map" peace plan to achieve peace and a Palestinian state by 2005. The Quartet, made up of the United States, European Union, Russia, and the United Nations, presented its plan to the Israeli government of Prime Minister Ariel Sharon, as well as to the Palestinian Authority President Mahmoud Abbas.[4, 5]

Both leaders had their own unique background. Sharon had been a platoon commander in the Alexandroni Brigade during the 1948 war for independence, having suffered combat wounds. He went on to achieve the rank of major and commanded the first Israeli special forces unit 101. There were accusations that this unit was used for tactical reprisals against Arab populations and many western nations condemned its actions including the United States. Now, in his latter days, he was a seasoned politician of the political right. But the pressure from Israel's great ally, the United States of America, was becoming too much to stand against. Shortly after the "road map" peace conference, bending to international pressure, Israel announced its qualified acceptance of the plan.[6]

On the other side of the negotiating table was Mahmoud Abbas. He had risen through the ranks of the Palestinian Liberation Organization headed by Yasser Arafat. Abbas had entered graduate studies in Moscow where his thesis, completed in 1982, was called "The Secret Connection between the Nazis and the Leaders of the Zionist Movement." The thesis argued that the Jews were working in concert with the Nazis for their own extermination. In another of his writings concerning the Holocaust, he declared, "Many scholars have debated the figure of six million and reached stunning conclusions---fixing the number of Jewish victims at only a few hundred thousand."

Abbas would go on, in other writings, to point out that "the Zionist movement led a broad campaign of incitement against the Jews living under Nazi rule to arouse the government's hatred of them, to fuel vengeance against them and to expand the mass extermination." He has also been accused of raising the money that supported the terrorist attack in Munich at the 1972 Summer Olympics. Mahmoud Abbas is considered a moderate Palestinian leader, and it is his "moderation" that led to the international support which finally brought him to power.[7]

As these two leaders met with the representatives of the Quartet, much blood had been spilled on both sides of the abyss over the years. In the last 31 months of violence, more than 2,000 Palestinians and 700 Israelis had been killed. With little hope for an improvement in that situation, the gathering of powers under the Quartet placed the onus on President Abbas to rein in the Palestinian militants conducting car bombings and suicide attacks that were responsible for the escalation of violence, and increasing deaths. Yet, in spite of the international effort to restore order and bring peace to the region, on April 30, just as the conference was opening, Shaikh Ahmed Yassin, the spiritual leader of the Palestinian Islamist group Hamas, vowed that the attacks would continue and that his group rejected the "road map." During his announcement, Yassin gladly took responsibility for a suicide bomb attack carried out in Tel Aviv on April 29, where three innocent people were murdered.[8]

The goal of the "road map" was to achieve a comprehensive settlement of the Israeli-Palestinian conflict by establishing a Palestinian state. This state would be located in the West Bank area where most Palestinians lived, known in ancient times as Judea. Judea had within its borders the ancient Israeli cities of Nazareth, Bethlehem, and Bethany, all of Biblical fame.

Judea's storied history also included the city revered by the three major religions of the world, Jerusalem. All of Judea was captured during the Six-Day War in 1967, after the lightning strike by Israel against the gathering armies of Syria, Jordan, and Egypt, quickly hitting them before they could strike first. As in ancient times, the Jews of Israel scored an amazing victory against much larger armies. This, too, led many Biblical, and Torah scholars to consider the ancient words of such prophets as Ezekiel, who had predicted the return of the nation of Israel to this land, including the Holy city of Jerusalem. In the ancient Hebrew Scriptures, chapter 36 of Ezekiel indicated:

> *Therefore say unto the house of Israel, thus saith the Lord GOD; I do not this for your sakes, O house of Israel, but for mine holy name's sake, which ye have profaned among the heathen...* Then, two verses later: *For I will take you from among the heathen, and gather you out of all countries, and will bring you into your own land.*[9]

At 10:00 A.M. on April 30 2003, President George Bush entered the White House Rose Garden to deliver his vision of the Quartet's "road map." He "spoke of a day when two states, Israel and Palestine, will live side by side in peace and security." As Israel's biggest and strongest supporter, the President applied the pressure:

> [T]he government of Israel, as the terror threat is removed and security improves, must take concrete steps to support the emergence of a viable and credible Palestinian state... settlement activity in the occupied territories must end.[10]

The words might as well have come from a nine-hundred pound

gorilla. The United States had become so essential to the existence of Israel, that to alienate any American government was no longer an Israeli option. Now, with the United States squarely in the corner of removing the lands given to Israel by God Himself, the Israeli government had a dilemma. Give up the lands and become vulnerable to destruction by fanatic enemies on every side, or stand firm and have a problem with its greatest ally. In addition to the more practical political and military concerns, there was another issue of great concern for Jews of faith.

So many of the ancient scriptures telling of a time when Israel would return to the "Promised Land" had been fulfilled, that any turning away from the land was now unthinkable. Yet, the pressure was indeed great. Each year the United States provided billions of dollars in assistance both militarily and economically. Should this help be discontinued by an American government not pleased with Israel, the consequences would be severe.[11]

With U.S. foreign policy clearly stated earlier that morning, the conference began. The Quartet issued a statement approved by all four of its members to both the Israeli and Palestinian delegations. The statement was in line with President Bush's vision of two states, but with something added. After declaring the need for the land of Judea to be given to the Palestinians for their own state, it went on to say what it expected, and required, from the Israeli government:

> Israeli leadership [shall] issue(s) an unequivocal statement affirming its commitment to the two-state vision of an independent, viable, sovereign Palestinian state...[12][13]

Now, it is one thing to lead a man to the gallows, but to require him to come in agreement with the hangman is entirely another matter. Israel was now required to agree with the removal of the land that now served as a buffer of protection against her enemies.

THE WORST WEATHER IN U.S. HISTORY

As the Quartet's conference for the "road map" was being kicked off, another event in United States also began. April 30, 2003 saw the beginning of tornados in the mid-section of the U.S. A total of twenty-one struck the states of Colorado, Iowa, Illinois, Mississippi, and Kansas. In the next three days, twenty-nine tornados struck Nebraska, New York, Oklahoma, Indiana, South Carolina, Texas and South Dakota. On May 4, Kansas, Nebraska, South Dakota, Mississippi, Illinois, Kentucky, Tennessee, and Arkansas were riveted by eighty-five tornados!

Also, on May 4, a very powerful F4 tornado touched down in southwest Madison County, Tennessee. Initially, it was reported to be between 200 and 300 yards in diameter. However, as the funnel approached the town of Jackson, it intensified into a half mile-wide monster that plowed through downtown Jackson destroying or damaging hundreds of buildings and homes. Another powerful F4 tornado hit north Kansas City. This storm reached 500 yards in diameter and leveled even the strongest buildings in its path. The next day twenty-one tornados hit seven states, followed by seventy-five tornados hitting on May 6 in thirteen states.[14] On May 8, in Moore, Oklahoma, the local McDonald's "swing manager," Carol Battaglia, was working her shift. The day started off like any other, but before it was over, it would leave a lasting memory for her and the town. That afternoon, news reports began to circulate about a tornado forming just outside town. As the clouds overhead began to look ominous, Battaglia started planning what she and the staff would do if the twister came their way. That planning would prove timely. As two families with children were in the McDonald's Play Place, a play room surrounded with a large glass window, Battaglia immediately asked them to leave. Battaglia had just decided that the men's bathroom would be the safest place in the facility, when a patron spotted the tornado. The storm was almost upon them, striking a church only a short block away. Immediately, everyone on the premises crowded into the men's bathroom, thirteen in all, just before the twister's fury struck. Moments later everyone could hear the roar and breaking glass as it passed over, ripping off the roof. Thankfully, nobody was injured except for Battaglia, who suffered a minor eye injury that would soon heal.[15]

Mother Nature wasn't finished yet. Over the course of the next four days one hundred fifty-eight more tornados ravaged twenty-one states. From April 30, the day it all began, through the fourth week of May, a record-breaking five hundred sixty-two tornados were reported! The previous record was three hundred ninety-nine tornados in June 1992. The previous record was broken by over 30%! That May also distinguished itself in the tornado record books for the most in the first twelve days of any month, three hundred fifty-four, shattering the previous record of one hundred ninety-six by more than 80%![16]

Based on U.S. storm records, weather experts described the Midwest weather events that began on April 30, 2003 and continuing through May as "the worst weather in United States history!"[17] As if 562 tornados were not enough, 1,587 hail storms were also recorded as well as 740 reports of wind damage. There is no record in United States history pertaining to a time of severe weather that comes close to the weather that started on April 30, 2003 just as the doors to the "peace" conference to remove the "Promised Land" from Israel officially opened.[18]

CHAPTER ELEVEN

The Great European Heat Wave

The Treaties of Rome were an accomplishment that few Europeans ever imagined would actually happen, with unity finally coming to the nations of Europe for the first time since the days of Charlemagne, and before that, the Roman Empire.[1] With the beginnings of unity came the hope that the centuries of warfare between the nations of Europe would finally come to an end. Warfare had been the norm, rather than the exception throughout the long and storied history of the European continent. The most destructive of the wars came in the 20th century, with millions dead in World War One.[2] Then, horribly more millions died a short 22 years later with World War Two.[3] The wartime alliances of the European nations would change from time to time, but one thing remained constant. The centuries of intrigue and politics had established an unrelenting fear on the continent that one European power would achieve military dominance and, thus, economic dominance over the rest of Europe.

This concern brought the British into the First World War on the side of France, against the forces of the German Kaiser in 1914. England entered the war to stop German dominance of the continent, even though the great moat, called the English Channel, was an almost impenetrable barrier of protection in that day. England would again fight on France's side in World War Two.[4] It was these two devastating wars that drained both the lives and treasuries of the warring European nations, and also acted as the catalyst behind the efforts of European leaders to create a peaceful and united Europe that the two treaties signed in Rome intended to bring about.

Recovery after the First World War came slowly. For the Western powers in that war, mainly Britain and France, victory had come at such a cost as to be indistinguishable from defeat. The war left an indelible mark on the politics of those nations in the years that followed, contributing in many ways to the next, even more devastating world war a generation later. However, on the other side of the battlefield, the German people were not only prostrate with exhaustion of every type, but also tasted the bitterness of defeat on a daily basis. With defeat also came draconian measures designed to extract every ounce of the pound of flesh that the British and French were demanding from those they believed left them no option but to fight in 1914.[5]

Against this backdrop brewed the elements of the next World War. With the victors promising never again, and the sons of Teutonic warriors vowing revenge, the stage was set. After the conclusion of the Second World War, proud Europe lay prostrate, divided between East and West. With Germany at the heart of the division, it would last some 50 years, with the Eastern part dominated by the Soviet Union's socialist police model, and its great potential lay dormant.[6]

Instead of the European nations playing the role of world powers, as they were historically accustomed to, they were now relegated to pawns in a game between two superpowers. But within the hearts and minds of the many leaders on the continent, mindful of Europe's grand history, there was only one hope. As the hundreds of Germanic states united under Frederick the Great, so, too, must Europe become united. So, in spite of the long history of hatred and war, amazingly, the Treaties of Rome were signed in 1957.[7]

The two treaties involved the nations of Belgium, France, Italy, Luxembourg, the Netherlands, and West Germany. They were initially confined to the establishment of the European Economic Community and the European Atomic Energy commission. In the years that followed the European Union evolved with the member nations eventually numbering twenty-seven. With almost five hundred million citizens, and thirty percent of the world's gross domestic product, the EU, as it began to be called, became an economic force to be reckoned with. The EU developed a single market through a standardized system of laws which applied in all member states, guaranteeing the freedom of movement of people, goods, services and capital. The E U also developed its own foreign policy, and along with that policy, its own foreign relations representative in the person of Javier Solana.[8] And this is where our story picks up.

EUROPE'S INVOLVEMENT

As a player on the world scene again, the European Union became involved in President Bush's "road map" to Middle East peace. Previously, the United States was the sole driving force behind the "land for peace" move. But now for the first time, the European Union would proudly play a major role. As a member of the Quartet, along with the U.S., Russia, and the U.N., Europe was now finally prepared to help move the peace process along between the Israelis and Palestinians. In the eyes of most diplomats, moving the peace process along meant removing the ancient "Promised Land" from Israel.

In discussions with Palestinian President Abbas, Solana noted, "I am very happy about the ideas and the steps that Mahmoud Abbas presented to us."[9] In a joint statement by the Quartet, the European Union noted that "a settlement agreed between the parties, will result in the emergence of an independent, democratic, and viable Palestinian state..."[10]

On April 30, 2003, as the Quartet's "road map" meeting began, President Bush pointed out that the United States had developed this plan in "close cooperation with the European Union, Russia, and the United Nations."[11] But the President was being kind. The much-ignored United Nations carried little clout and even less ability to gather the parties together. Russia, still recovering from the painful break-up of the Soviet Union, was not far behind the U.N. in that respect. As always had been the case, this was a show produced and directed by the United States. But now, for the first time, the U.S. had a strong partner in the effort to forge a peace agreement. The curtain rose on the emerging European Union to enter the international stage.[13][14]

The Quartet's suggested Palestinian state could only be created on the land that the ancient Hebrew Scriptures clearly indicated were given to Israel. Remembering the ancient words of the prophet Ezekiel in chapter 37:

> *And say unto them, Thus saith the Lord GOD; Behold, I will take the children of Israel from among the heathen, whither they be gone, and will gather them on every side, and bring them into their own land: And I will make them one nation in the land upon the mountains of Israel; and one king shall be king to them all: and they shall be no more two nations, neither shall they be divided into two kingdoms any more at all.*[14]

The Jews had been scattered among the nations for over two thousand years, and then returned to *their own land*. We know that these words were written some 2500 years ago. Part of the prophecy came true in 1948, and again in 1967 when more of the land was added during the Six-Day War.[15] But now the United States was not the only critical world player pressing the "land for peace" process that would remove part of the "Promised Land" from Israel. The European Union was now deeply engaged in the effort to remove this land from the Jewish nation and give it to their enemy.

As we know, when the United States launched the latest "land for peace" effort on April 30, 2003, the "worst weather in U.S. history" began its historical rampage on that same day. That conference pitted the United States, and now a revived Europe, against the ancient promises of God, according to the Hebrew Scriptures. The belief held by both the U.S. and E.U. was that true peace would result only if the land was given. But as the furious natural disturbances that struck the Midwest finally began to subside, in late May, another natural disturbance of historical significance and destruction was just beginning on the other side of the Atlantic Ocean.

THE GREAT HEAT WAVE

The weather in France varies according to the landscape. A traveler can go skiing in the Alps while a friend is resting on the sand beaches of Cannes. In the north-central part of France, from Paris south through the Loire River Valley, and then on to Bordeaux and the Bay of Biscay, the summer temperatures only average in the high 70s. This area is a place of great comfort for those wishing to escape the hotter parts of the world during the summer months. Along the southern Mediterranean coastline, the summers are notoriously mild and very comfortable. All of this has made France a top summer tourist destination, except in the years of World War Two.[16]

France has been the destination of many famous persons during the summer months. Winston Churchill traveled to Dreux, France, to the chateau of Consuelo Balsan to vacation in August 1939, just before the Second World War started. This represented a sort of last chance at refreshment in the blissful weather of France before the onset of that great struggle. But that was before the summer of 2003.[17]

As the 562 tornados and a wide assortment of additional weather grievances, known as the "worst weather in the history of the United States," was ending in May 2003, the European heat wave, known as the Great Drought, was just beginning. It would be one of the hottest summers on record in Europe. Temperature records were broken in a number of countries as some parts of Europe experienced their hottest weather in at least two hundred fifty years---since the British were still running the colonies in North America!

The unusually warm weather began in June and climaxed in the first two weeks of August. Crops withered. Rivers dried up. Fires started. Between July and mid-August the high temperatures ran 20 to 30 percent higher than the seasonal average. The heat was so severe that the mass of alpine glaciers in Switzerland decreased by up to 10% in 2003 alone.[18]

In France, many of the nuclear reactors are cooled by river water, which is then returned back to the river. But, in the summer of 2003, many of the rivers used in this process had water levels so low that the cooling process became impossible. Plants had to be shut down for safety reasons. This loss of electrical power happened at the worst time possible as the need for electricity to keep air conditioners going was critical.[19]

But as savaging as the weather was on the economy and crops, the death toll was what staggered the imagination. The numbers reached were unheard of, in western countries, from natural disasters. In France alone, 14,802 people died as a direct result of the heat wave, most of them elderly. Part of the reason for the terrible death toll was the lack of a contingency plan for such a weather related event. Although there were emergency procedures for a variety of catastrophes and natural events, the notion of needing one for extremely hot weather had not occurred to anyone in authority, and no emergency plan existed. It did not exist because it simply was never needed. No previous experience would have even brought the need for such a plan to the minds of the planners.[20] So France was unprepared. Gruesomely the death toll was so horrific that undertakers needed to use a refrigerated warehouse on the outskirts of Paris. Their own facilities simply lacked the necessary space.[21]

In Italy, nearly 3000 people died when temperatures held at very high levels for several weeks. The United Kingdom saw record high temperatures recorded and suffered a death toll of some 2,045 persons. London recorded its first triple-digit Fahrenheit temperature on August 10, and approximately 900 people died that day. In Belgium, temperatures higher than any recorded since 1833 resulted in 150 deaths, according to the Royal Meteorological Society. Germany suffered terribly, losing 7000 persons to the heat wave. With only half the usual rainfall, the rivers Elbe and Danube were un-navigable.[22][23][24]

In Switzerland, the melting of glaciers in the Alps resulted in avalanches and flash flooding, after decreasing the size of the glacier by 10%. Tragically, that summer would be the hottest since the year 1540, resulting in over 900 deaths from the extreme heat. With temperatures exceeding the average by 10 degrees Fahrenheit, the prevailing conditions in Geneva, Switzerland matched the usual summers in Rio de Janeiro.[25][26]

In Portugal, extensive forest fires destroyed 5% of the countryside and 10% of the forest, representing an area of 2500 square miles. Between Italy and Spain, some 4000 people were estimated to have died when temperatures exceeded 100 degrees Fahrenheit for weeks at a time. But since 2003, the Italian Institute of Statistics revealed that Italy might have suffered as many as 18,000 deaths attributable to the heat wave. The Institute estimates 9,700 fatalities within the month of August alone.[27][28][29]

CONCLUSION

After the heat wave finally ended, the extent of the catastrophe began to be revealed. Some estimates indicated that the tragic death toll reached as high as a staggering 52,000 Europeans, making it one of the greatest climate-related disasters in recorded Western history![30] The beginning of this disaster came in June 2003, immediately after the "worst weather in United States history had just ended." That weather in the U.S. began on the exact day that the Quartet's "road map" conference was launched, providing yet another "coincidence" for consideration.

The start of the April 30 Middle East peace conference also marked Europe's participation, as a major player, in the Middle East peace process for the first time. This effectively meant that the United States was now sharing the effort of forging some kind of peace agreement between the Palestinians and Israelis. But in a more real sense, this sharing of the effort meant Europe's deep involvement in brining about the removal of the ancient "Promised Land" from Israel for the creation of a Palestinian state.[31]

CHAPTER TWELVE

Hurricane Katrina

At the stroke of midnight something happened that was unthinkable until only recently. Armed Israeli forces began removing Jewish settlers from land that Biblically was considered a part of Israel. The date was August 15, 2005. The much dreaded move to evict Jewish settlers from the Gaza strip began with a warning from Israeli security forces that all settlers would have 48 hours to leave. *The Bible* makes reference to Gaza as the place where Samson was delivered into bondage by Delilah, and where he died while toppling the temple of the pagan god Dagon. As the clock stroked midnight, CNN reported:

> "Israeli officials planned to begin informing the approximately 8,500 Jewish settlers that they have 48 hours to leave Gaza or be removed by force. Some have already left."[1]

But not all of the 8500 settlers were willing to leave peaceably. Police reported rioting in Neve Dekalim, the largest of the settlements, with about 300 people involved.[2] Israeli leaders that had worked closely with President George W. Bush came under severe criticism for agreeing to leave the land. Vice Prime Minister Shimon Perez assured CNN, "I'm sure that history will justify our choice."[3]

Many settlers, as CNN reported, promised to resist. They were joined in Gaza by about 5000 "anti-withdrawal" activists. "We're going to have to tell the government, no you cannot take us out of Gush Katif," settler Rachel Saperstein said. "We are going to stay here as long as possible, as long as our food supply holds out, our water supply and beyond that."[4]

The Voice of America broadcast an individual story of a settler being removed on August 17, 2005:

> A settler, holding his young daughter -- lifted her up before a
> line of soldiers, screaming at them -- asking if they would evict
> her from her home. One of the soldiers briefly spoke with the
> man, but others stood motionless as he moved along.[5]

That day's edition of the *Jerusalem Post* editorialized that police and soldiers would "knock on the doors of ... citizens who have withstood almost five years of terrorism only to be evicted by their own government." But the *Post* went on to express the real concern many Israelis had on that day. They feared that the act of eviction, viewed as a betrayal by many, would result in violence of Jew against Jew. "Indeed, though our enemies are rejoicing at the suffering of the settlers, they will rejoice even more if we decide to tear ourselves apart," the *Post* added.[6, 7, 8]

The Palestinian side drew a different perspective on the unilateral Israeli withdraw. Mahmoud Zahhar, a senior Hamas official told the London-based newspaper *Al-Sharq al-Awsat,*

> ...the resistance must move to the West Bank to drive out the oc-
> cupation. We will not take the Gaza Strip and flee to a state of calm
> and tranquility while the Zionist enemy continues to detain thou-
> sands of our sons, and while it occupies the West Bank.[9]

GAZA REMOVAL FORETOLD?

There is, however, another perspective relating to the removal of the Jews from Gaza worth considering. That perspective, given by a man named Zephaniah, who lived between 686 and 643 B.C., appears to have foretold the Gaza evictions. Zephaniah was considered a prophet of God by the ancient Jews, and his writings are recorded in the Old Testament of the Bible. His ministry was credited with a great revival that spread over Judah in his time. But it is what he wrote relating to Gaza that is of significance here. In talking about a time in the distant future, where nations will gather against Israel, he refers to some specific events that would take place. In Chapter 2 of the Book of Zephaniah:

> *For Gaza shall be forsaken, and Ashkelon a desolation: they shall drive out Ashdod at the noon day, and Ekron shall be rooted up.*[10]

This prophet says that the Jews will "forsake" Gaza at some future date. That general time is well in the future as is noted in the "Dake" annotated reference Bible. Therefore, this "forsaking" Gaza could not have been fulfilled in the past, but only after the modern rebirth of the state of Israel.[11]

Zephaniah also spoke about the Israeli city of Ashkelon, just outside of Gaza. Somehow, it would become desolate. According to Webster's dictionary, "desolate" means "to deprive of inhabitants, to lay waste, forsake, or to make wretched." This brings us to the current events happening in that city, as reported in 2007 from *Haaretz News:*

> A shopping mall in Ashkelon was hit yesterday afternoon by a long-range rocket fired from the Gaza Strip injuring around 90 people, four of them seriously. Two militant groups, Islamic Jihad and the Popular Resistance Committees, claimed responsibility.[12]

In fact, as the article indicates, Ashkelon has come under Hamas rocket fire. The city is well within range of the rockets Hamas had trained on it. The *Haaretz News* report indicated that 90 people were injured by one rocket.[13] A multitude of rockets could cause that city to become "desolate," especially if Hamas begins tipping them with something more lethal than high explosives, like poisonous gas or chemicals. Any city under such a reign of terror is not a good place to raise families, or settle in for retirement, not knowing if your dedicated neighbor will finally succeed in making it your last day.

In the January/February 1998 publication *Archaeology*, the Archaeological Institute of America, noted that the ancient Israeli city of Ekron was found in recent years. The writings of Zephaniah indicate that *Ekron shall be rooted up.* Since its relatively recent discovery, Ekron is in fact getting rooted up by archaeologists.[14]

As the Palestinians consolidated their control over Gaza, the range and accuracy of their rocket attacks continued to grow. Eventually, in late December 2008, after over 5000 rockets had slammed into Israel, the Israeli Defense Forces launched a full scale incursion into Gaza to rid militant forces of their ability to attack. On January 10, 2009, *Haaretz News* service in Israel would report rockets reaching the ancient city of Ashdod, deeper within Israel.[15] As the militant rocket attacks grow in sophistication, destructiveness, and accuracy, the need of the citizens of Ashdod to evacuate to shelters is probably not far off. Thus *they shall drive out Ashdod at the noon day* may have been referring to citizens fleeing to air raid shelters for protection against rocket attacks.

The words of Zephaniah appear to be describing events relating to four places relatively close to one another, Gaza, Ashkelon, Ekron, and Ashdod. Each prophecy mirrors an unfolding of events in the present day.

KATRINA

On August 23, 2005, the same day that Israeli officials declared the removal of the Jews from Gaza officially complete, something else on the other side of the world was just beginning. Near the Bahamas, tropical depression number twelve was noticed by the National Weather Service for the first time. The next day it strengthened to a tropical storm and was named Katrina. Then, it proceeded to make landfall in the southern tip of Florida as a minimal hurricane.[16]

In passing across Florida, Katrina weakened to a tropical storm; however, the warm waters of the Gulf of Mexico allowed it to rapidly intensify to the sixth strongest Atlantic hurricane in recorded history. Once in the Gulf, the storm's computer model projected it to hit the City of New Orleans sometime on Monday, August 29.

A CNN report early that day described the expectations for New Orleans. They were extreme, with the winds produced by the storm expected to "drive a wall of water over the city's levees." With 70 percent of the city below sea level, and protected from the Mississippi River by another section of levees, the city lay at the mercy of nature. Now, with the approach of the storm, conditions were already deteriorating. Nine hours later, at landfall, the worst would be upon the "city that care forgot." The Big Easy, known for its laid-back party atmosphere that drew thousands of tourists annually, would soon be changed forever. With Katrina packing winds of 160 mph, fear began to grip the city.[17]

"This is the threat we've never faced before," said Mayor Ray Nagin. With a mandatory evacuation in place, most of the 1.1 million people who lived in New Orleans and its suburbs had started evacuating over the last few days. Storm tracks predicted Katrina would hit the city in a potential worst-case scenario. By Sunday night, over one million people had fled the city. Between 20,000 and 25,000 others who remained took up shelter at the soon to be infamous Super Dome. "This is a biggie," said Steve Rinard, meteorologist in charge of the National Weather Service office in Lake Charles, Louisiana. "We've been dreading a storm like this."[18]

After the storm hit, damage assessments began to account for the great destruction that had just been visited upon the city. It was severe. But before the day was over, a stunning development would unfold, turning what was already the most damaging hurricane in U.S. history, into a catastrophically destructive storm. Levees designed to protect the city began to break. As several levees gave way to the pressure of holding back so much water, the city began to fill with the murky waters of Lake Pontchartrain. Soon, most neighborhoods in the city had water inundating houses up their roof tops.

Katrina made landfall as a Category 3 storm near the Mississippi/ Louisiana border and would become the most expensive natural disaster in recorded history costing over $100 billion. The degree of harm Katrina accomplished is hard to overstate. It removed over 1,000,000 people from their homes, with many survivors climbing on to their roof tops to escape the rising waters. People had to be taken away by military personnel and bussed to cities, primarily in Texas. Though they would eventually be allowed to visit their home town in the months ahead, many would never live there again.[19]

CONCLUSION

Katrina, as with the other unusual disasters, occurred during the actions to remove land from Israel. With the removal of the Jews from some of these restored lands, countless Americans were removed from their homes and lands in an act of God of Biblical proportions. All of this coincided with the official ending of the Gaza removal. The end of one event, August 23, marked the beginning of the other, August 23.

However, the impact of Katrina went well beyond the destruction of New Orleans. It also marked the beginning of a general decline in the Presidency of George W. Bush. Scathing criticism was directed against the president by the media, stating that his response to the cataclysmic suffering from Katrina was too slow. Whether that criticism was justified or not is for historians to debate. From that point in his presidency, however, Bush's popularity began a slide of historic proportions from which he never rebounded. With poll numbers in the low 20s at times, his effectiveness as a leader was greatly diminished. Only President Richard Nixon, under impeachment threat, experienced unpopularity to that degree. By the 2008 elections, Bush was so unpopular that any politician attached to him paid for it at the polls.

In late 2008, near the end of the Bush Presidency, two top presidential aides would finally come out to discuss the impact of Katrina on the Bush Presidency. According to Matthew Dowd, Bush's pollster and chief strategist for the 2004 campaign:

> The president broke his bond with the public. Once that bond was broken, he no longer had the capacity to talk to the American public. State of the Union addresses? It didn't matter. Legislative initiatives? It didn't matter. P.R.? It didn't matter. Travel? It didn't matter.[20]

The other aid former White House communications director and counselor to the president Dan Bartlett, observed, "Politically it was the final nail in the coffin." For Bush, who had engineered the successful removal of a portion of the "Promised Land" from the Jews, the natural disaster of Katrina resulted in his own political disaster as well.[21] If there is another instance in American history of a natural disaster marking the historical decline of a presidency, it is not easily found.

On the other side of the world, Bush's partner in removing a portion of the "Promised Land" saw a fate that was even less kind. On January 3, 2006, a little more than four months after engineering the withdrawal from the Biblical lands he had sworn to keep, Ariel Sharon suffered a massive stroke.[22] Completely incapacitated, he lost not only the powerful office he held, but also his health. His last significant policy act as Prime Minister was the removal of land that Ezekiel prophesized would be returned to Israel, and referred to over the centuries as the "Promised Land."

The official date that the removal of the Jews from the "Promised Land" was completed marked the exact day Katrina was observed for the first time, destined to remove many from their homes. Was this timing a Divine effort to help mankind connect the dots of his actions? If it was, it was to no avail. Not long after the Gaza withdrawal, the effort against the ancient promise would accelerate, led by a powerful international group of four.[23]

CHAPTER THIRTEEN

Global Financial Meltdown

P roponents of the Israeli withdrawal from Gaza in August 2005 believed that such a move would lessen tensions in the area and create an atmosphere conducive for the peace process to move forward. They also believed it would begin to create some goodwill inside the Palestinian community, or at least lessen the deep distrust of Israel that seldom went far below the surface. In theory, it was believed by proponents that, after seeing the withdrawal of Israeli forces, Palestinians in Gaza would turn their attention to building the homeland they had so vehemently been protesting to attain. Instead, after the withdrawal was completed, the Palestinian Islamist group Hamas quickly began using its control of the area to dramatically increase the firing of Kassam rockets into Israel.[1]

The advantage of the Kassam missile is its size. Being a small rocket, it is exceedingly difficult to detect before it is fired. Typically, it is hidden in a commercial truck, set up in 15 minutes, and then fired. Then the truck disappears. The Kassam was first fired into Israeli towns near Gaza in April 2001. The firings were typically indiscriminately aimed into civilian areas in the hope of killing people and damaging property. 281 such attacks were recorded in 2004. In 2005, with the Israeli withdrawal imminent, the attacks tapered off to "only" 179. For the Israeli towns, such as ancient Ashkelon and Ashdod, that were within the rockets' reach, there appeared a momentary hope that the impending withdrawal from Gaza was beginning to produce some rare Middle East peace. But, after the Palestinians consolidated their control over the vacated area, a 500% increase in rocket attacks followed the next year, including assaults against Israeli towns that were not considered disputed territory by Israel's Arab neighbors.[2]

Then, in July 2007, Hamas would take complete control of Gaza from the Palestinian Authority in an act of armed rebellion against Fatah, the organization previously headed by Yasser Arafat.[3] With Gaza now squarely in the hands of Hamas, the smuggling of rockets increased significantly. The main reason for the increase appeared to be the Israeli loss of control over the Philadelphi route between the Gaza Strip and the Egyptian Sinai. After Israel withdrew its troops, this route became available for the importation of rockets, and Hamas was able to increase both the quality and quantity of its arsenal. As such, Hamas was able to use rockets with a greater range than anything it had previously possessed, and to target Ashkelon, an Israeli city of 120,000. Ashkelon was repeatedly struck by Katyusha rockets in late February 2008.

Prior to the 2005 Gaza withdrawal the number of rocket attacks against Israeli towns rarely reached 50 in a month. But, since 2006, Hamas had the ability to launch 50 in a day.

The Philadelphi route was captured from the Egyptians during the 1967 Six-Day War, when victorious Israeli forces took control of the Sinai desert.[4] Before the war, Egypt used the Sinai as a launching ground to invade Israel. But in 1967, after Israel's quick and substantial victory, the Sinai would become a buffer between it and the Egyptian army, and Israel was determined to retain this protection. In 1979, however, President Jimmy Carter was able to convince both nations to come together in an effort to make peace at Camp David. That effort paid off and on March 26, 1979, Sinai was returned to Egypt. In exchange Israel received diplomatic recognition from Egypt, and promises of peaceful coexistence, the same promises that awaited it from the Syrians, Palestinians, and the entire Arab world in exchange for the ancient "Promised Land."

The Camp David agreement had very specific language requiring each country to look out for the security of the other. Under Article III, Paragraph 2 of the treaty each party promised to:

> ...undertake(s) to refrain from organizing, instigating, inciting, assisting or participating in acts or threats of belligerency, hostility, subversion or violence against the other Party, anywhere, and undertakes to ensure that perpetrators of such acts are brought to justice.[5]

With a massive amount of deadly rockets coming across the Egyptian border on a regular basis, destined to be fired at Israel, it appeared that controlling its border was a task Egypt was not up to. Since the Israeli withdrawal from Gaza, smuggling across the border had grown by more than 300%. After the Gaza withdrawal, U.S. Secretary of State Condoleezza Rice worked out the "Rafah Crossing Agreement"[6] designed to regulate the Gaza-Egyptian Border. In this agreement, the European Union supplied third-party monitors to prevent the flow of weapons or cash to terrorist organizations inside Gaza. Frequently these monitors would have to leave their posts as the situation in the area deteriorated, leaving the route open for smugglers. But the main reason the border was a smuggling sieve was Egypt. So lax was Egypt's concern for the terms of the Camp David agreement that, in one instance, it had allowed Hamas terrorist operatives to travel to Tehran to be trained by the Islamic Revolutionary Guards, and then allowed them to return to Gaza. Essentially, they were allowed to receive their Masters' degrees in terrorism and return.

Having experienced an unrelenting barrage of rocket attacks in the last six years, coming from the now Palestinian controlled Gaza, on March 1, 2008, Israel launched a military incursion into Gaza in an attempt to destroy the rocket bases there. In all, over 3000 rocket attacks had been launched during those six years, with 45% hitting the Israeli town Sderot. But now, something happened that bordered on the bizarre.[7]

Sometimes life can be stranger than fiction, and this appears to be one of those moments. What is truly bizarre is a nation taking six years, and absorbing 3000 rocket attacks, before it retaliates. Perhaps another example of such national restraint can be found, but it won't be easy. The apparent reason for this restraint, or abdication of responsibility, appears to be the enormity of pressure placed on Israel to do nothing that might upset the "land for peace" process, where defending against Palestinian attacks was viewed negatively.

Whatever the reason, such a lack of response on the part of any nation being attacked is rare. But then, something happened to top it. UN Secretary-General Ban Ki-moon, who appeared over the years to have lost his voice when it came to criticism of the rocket attacks into Israel, found it in time to denounce the Israeli incursion as, "disproportionate and excessive use of force." The European Union President chimed in using essentially the same language to criticize Israeli efforts to stop rocket attacks against its civilian population.[8]

One might have thought these institutions would have applauded the degree of restraint that Israel exercised over the years of absorbing the attacks, restraint that, undoubtedly, the critics would have found difficult to possess under similar circumstances. But if either entertained such thoughts, there is no record of it. These criticisms, however, appeared to reveal a deeper problem within the United Nations and the European Union. Both had become anti-Semitic over the years, placing the concept of removing the ancient lands from the Jewish state above any safety concerns for its citizens.[9]

THE QUARTET

With the "progress" of the 2005 Israeli withdrawal, President Bush sought to add to that "success" by restarting the "road map" process. The goal was for more Israeli withdrawals to take place so a peace that had eluded the efforts of presidents since Truman would finally come to the troubled region. The Quartet had not met since 2003, and its "road map" peace process was pronounced dead by European Union diplomats as recently as 2006. But in November 2007, four years after the last Quartet conference, the group of four powers agreed to meet again in Annapolis, Maryland, at the United States Naval Academy. This meeting would represent a breakthrough in the effort to forge a Middle East peace agreement. The framework centered on trading portions of the "Promised Land" for various solemn promises from Israel's Arab enemies. The breakthrough would come as a result of the man that the Quartet had just appointed as its new envoy.[10] On June 27, 2007, Tony Blair, who hours earlier had just stepped down as Prime Minister of Great Brittan, announced he would spearhead the Quartet's Middle East peace effort. Never before had the Quartet been represented by such a prominent and respected envoy. In his farewell speech to parliament on that day, Blair summed up his guiding belief of his new role:

> The absolute priority is to try to give effect to what is now the consensus across the international community – that the only way of bringing stability and peace to the Middle East is a two-state solution.[11]

The goal for the conference, as noted by its host President Bush, was to restart the Quartet "road map" peace process. Due to the efforts of Blair, the conference this time would be a huge success. Blair was able to bring together not just the warring parties, but a multitude of nations to attend the conference with all participants essentially possessing the same goal; Israel must trade part of the "Promised Land" for a peace treaty.

When the conference finally convened, it was attended by members of the Quartet, consisting of the United States, European Union, United Nations and Russia, and also members of the Group of Eight Nations, plus more than a dozen Arab nations and numerous non-Arab nations as well. In total, 45 countries and international organizations from across the world were invited to attend Annapolis. They were: Algeria, Arab League, Bahrain, Brazil, Canada, China, Egypt, EU Commission, EU High Rep, EU President, France, Germany, Greece, India, Indonesia, Iraq, Italy, Japan, Jordan, Lebanon, Malaysia, Mauritania, Morocco, Norway, Oman, Pakistan, Poland, Qatar, Russia, Saudi Arabia, Senegal, Slovenia, South Africa, Spain, Sudan, Sweden, Syria, Quartet Envoy Blair, Tunisia, Turkey, UAE, United Kingdom, UNSYG, Yemen, and of course the United States.[12, 13]

For the first time in history the effort to forge a Middle East peace agreement had gone global. Never before had so many nations of the world come together in an effort to establish a framework to resolve the Arab-Israeli dispute. The new Quartet envoy, Blair, summed up the U.S. Administration's new attitude in the peace process saying, "You can debate about how much America put into this [land for peace process] a few years ago, but today President Bush and Secretary of State Condoleezza Rice are absolutely up for it."[14] But the main component of any settlement between the Israelis and Palestinians would still be the removal of large parts of Judea and Samaria, the ancient "Promised Land." The conference would convene November 27, 2007.

Jews in opposition to the conference and what it would ultimately do began gathering in Jerusalem and organized into mass demonstrations that marched to the U.S. Consulate as a meeting was taking place there among members of the Quartet. The meeting was part of the preparations for the Annapolis Conference scheduled later that month. In attendance were Secretary of State Rice, Israeli Prime Minister Olmert and Quartet envoy Tony Blair. The goal of their meeting was to establish a "declaration of principals" to be presented at the November 27, 2007 conference. Those principals would ultimately espouse trading the ancient "Promised Land" in exchange for promises from the Palestinians, and the Arab nations surrounding Israel, that they would stop trying to destroy her. Assurances would be granted guaranteeing Israel that, if attacked, she would be assisted by the international community. Strangely, Israeli citizens appeared unimpressed by these promises.

Knesset Member Uri Ariel told reporters from the rally, "We're telling Olmert: Stop selling the land of Israel, do not divide Jerusalem, do not even think of destroying Jewish towns, the land of Israel belongs to us, to the people of Israel. You have no mandate for this." Likud Member Steinitz denounced plans to divide Jerusalem saying, "Ehud [Olmert], Ehud [Barak], and Tzipi[Livni] are deceiving the entire people and leading us to the Annapolis trap while ignoring the facts on the ground."[15] Protestors angrily decried that a return to the pre-1967 borders made Israel vulnerable to attack from the nations surrounding her. Such borders were described by the late Labor party leader, Abba Eban, as the "Auschwitz borders"[16] named after the famous death camp that Hitler's Third Reich had used to exterminate countless Jews during the Second World War.

An *Al Jazeera* Arab news correspondent in Cairo observed, "We expect every single country invited to attend. But, every country wants something in return. For example, Syria wants to mention the right to regain Golan, which was occupied by Israel in 1967."[17]

The conference was to be a "Promised Land" bazaar with the land promised in ancient Hebrew Scriptures exchanged for promises of peace from enemies that had attempted to extinguish the life of the Jewish nation on more than one occasion. Those attempts ultimately failed, ironically, resulting in the restoration of more of these ancient "Promised

Lands" to Israel. Now, the world was coming together in the effort to remove these lands in the name of peace.

Such a peace between Israel and an Arab enemy where polls still showed an overwhelming majority of Palestinians refused to accept the existence of the Jewish nation. Also, a peace where Palestinian schools taught eight year old children that Israel was an enemy to be slaughtered, not accepted.[18] Should the "Promised Lands" bazaar the world was now holding succeed in removing Samaria and Judea from Israel, the widest part of the nation, from the Mediterranean Sea to the border of a newly-created Palestinian state, would be sixty miles wide, while the narrowest part would only be three miles. From a military viewpoint, this would make the mid-section of the nation a prime target in any future Arab attack, with the nation being able to be easily split in two. An army from the new Palestinian state could attack at the narrowest point, then after advancing three miles, the nation foretold by Ezekiel would be cut in two and vulnerable to extermination.[19]

After the Annapolis Conference, representatives of Israel and the Palestinian Authority would meet on a regular basis, working to resolve differences on a wide range of issues with the ultimate goal being a comprehensive peace agreement.

The next conference was held in Sharm El-Sheikh, Egypt, on November 8, 2008. At that conference, after taking stock of the year of negotiations begun at Annapolis, Secretary of State Rice observed what all present knew to be true, that "the distance to peace has been narrowed although peace has not been achieved." She said this after meeting Palestinian leader Abbas during her 19th visit to the Middle East in two years, and she went on to point out that Annapolis had laid the foundation that ultimately would establish the state of Palestine.

With the participation of the global community, for the first time in the history of the Arab-Israeli dispute, substantial progress was made toward a peace settlement between Israel and the Palestinians. This potentially watershed development began taking shape only after a man of significant stature, Former British Prime Minister Blair, took over as Quartet envoy. After his appointment as envoy on June 27, 2007, progress began almost immediately. On July 23, 2007, Blair headed to the Middle East for the first time as the Quartet's point man. He would remain there for five days visiting the various parties, with success that would soon translate into the Annapolis Conference the following November. Then that conference would translate into an "understanding" between the warring parties.[20, 21]

Finally, on December 10, 2008, a report in *Israel Today* indicated significant breakthroughs in the "land for peace" negotiations after Annapolis.[22] This success came only after the international community began uniting behind Blair, beginning on his first trip to the troubled region as the newly appointed Quartet envoy on July 23, 2007.[23, 24] That date would, therefore, mark the beginning of the new Quartet effort, where the group of four political powers would begin again to wield their considerable influence to remove a portion of the ancient lands from the Israelites. The negotiations that began on July 23, 2007 were so significant that in 2009, Blair was quoted again in the Jerusalem-based *Israel Today,* saying that "continuous meetings between Abbas and Olmert...have produced an agreement," but based on their wishes, the details would be kept secret for the time being."[25] Pressure from the Quartet and the international community appeared to make the difference, with breakthroughs that established a framework for the parties to move the process forward. If Blair's estimation was correct, sometime in the foreseeable future, Judea and Samaria would no longer be under Israeli rule.

GLOBAL FINANCIAL EARTHQUAKE

Although the Annapolis Conference met in late November 2007, Tony Blair's effort to pull together the conference began on July 23, 2007 with the launching of his first trip to the Middle East. The agenda of the

Conference centered on separating the "Promised Land" from Israel, in exchange for promises from the surrounding Arab countries that they would become good neighbors once the lands were given up. But it was no longer only the United States involved in this effort. Now many nations from across the globe had become active in the process. With a multitude of nations gathered in this common cause, pressure on Israel to give up the land so necessary to her survival was now extreme. The success at Annapolis, and, particularly, its aftermath, would be noted by U.S. Secretary of State Rice and Quartet envoy Tony Blair. It was, however, during this time frame that the nations of the world experienced what economists and the media have called the most serious global financial crisis since the Great Depression. As of August 2009, the crisis was far from over in spite of massive and coordinated efforts by central banks across the world to prop up critical financial institutions.

The financial earthquake that began rocking the world in 2007 was, in a sense, comparable to a physical earthquake. The elements of destruction existed under the surface prior to the event. But, it is the actual earthquake event that is remembered, not the building up of pressure that would inevitably release its dire consequences. Once the earthquake begins, it indiscriminately takes down what were believed to be sturdy structures. So did the financial earthquake that began shaking the world and revealing itself in 2007. The aftershocks, throughout 2008 and 2009, would continue to heighten in their intensity, creating a climate of financial distrust and outright fear as great financial structures, once thought unshakable, began to crumble. But there is another comparison between the physical earthquake and financial one that can be made. Both had an epicenter. In the case of the financial earthquake, now being called the Global Financial Meltdown, that epicenter was interbank lending. Lending between banks, critical to the functioning of the international banking system, quite suddenly froze.

The lifeblood of the international banking system is liquidity, available cash on hand for banks to meet all of their legal obligations to depositors. Since available funds within banks vary from day to day, based on withdrawals versus deposits, a bank will often have a surplus of liquidity available for lending in the overnight interbank system, where banks lend to other banks. On the other hand, when depositor withdrawals and other immediate obligations exceed available cash, that same bank will then enter the interbank lending system to borrow the necessary funds to meet immediate obligations. As with all lending activities, the creditworthiness of the bank is the key factor in determining its participation in these interbank lending transactions and determines what the premium charged for its overnight borrowing will be. Fear about a bank's creditworthiness would not only result in depositors withdrawing funds, but also in that bank's inability to tap the interbank lending system. This inability to accomplish short-term borrowing creates an even more unstable bank and one that is unlikely to survive as access to funds is cut off.

There is, however, a method of measuring how banks view the risk of lending to each other on a system-wide international banking basis. It is called the Libor-OIS spread.[26] To sum it up, this spread represents the premium charged by banks to lend short term, uncollateralized funds to other banks overnight. Like an auto insurance policy, the greater the perceived risk, the higher the premium charged. It is that simple. Alan Greenspan told Bloomberg Financial news in February 2009, that the "Libor-OIS spread remains a barometer of fears of bank insolvency." This premium charged, by banks to banks, is measured in 100ths of one percent and has averaged, between 2001 and July 2007, between 6/100ths and 8/100ths of one percent.[27] Essentially, the small premium indicated that, within the international banking community, there was very little concern about the solvency of banks participating in this interbank lending system.

This sense of security was an ingrained feature of the international banking community, creating significant economic benefits to borrowers worldwide. Since the premium being paid was so low, banks had only a small added interest expense to their own interest charges for the end user, the borrower. Additionally, the possibility of a bank getting caught short on critical funds overnight was almost nonexistent. That was, however, until July 2007.

That same week the new Quartet envoy, Tony Blair, began his maiden voyage to the Middle East to gather support for the Annapolis Conference, something began to go terribly wrong with the worldwide banking system. On July 26, three days after Blair's trip began, the risk premium paid by banks to banks jumped over 50% from what it had averaged over the course of the prior month, reaching almost 13/100ths of a percent. That one-day jump, in itself, was unusual, but did not threaten the international banking system. It did, however, represent a significant increase in the perceived risk that banks across the world believed they were taking by lending funds in the overnight money market to one another.[28, 29]

Unfortunately, the July 26 jump in the premium would prove to be more than a one day anomaly. Instead, it would mark the beginning of an historical rise in the interbank risk premium, representing growing fear within banking circles that would, ultimately, bring the international banking system to the brink of a systemic collapse. Over the course of the next several days, the risk premium would continue to increase hitting an unheard of 48/100ths of a percent on August 10. Significant fear was gripping banks worldwide. By September 2007, the premium would reach an incredible 94/100ths of one percent, an eleven fold increase over its previous average! The impact of this banking fear was immediately felt throughout the world's financial markets.

By September 2008, both bank-to-bank and bank-to-consumer lending would become almost completely frozen. By October 10, 2008, the risk premium would hit the dizzying height of 364/100ths! But, this incredibly high premium would only have to be paid if a bank could be found to lend at that rate. At "UniCredit Markets and Investment Banking" in Munich, strategist Kornelius Purps described the crisis, "This is unheard of, the money markets should be the engine driving the financial system, but they have broken down."[30, 31, 32, 33] Christopher Rieger, a strategist at the market trading company "Dresdner Kleinwort" in Frankfurt, Germany would describe it this way: "The money markets have completely broken down with no trading taking place at all...there is no market any more. Central banks are the only providers of cash to the market, no one else is lending."

Those closest to the action began to fear that the banking problem was even too big for world governments, and their central banks, to fix. At ABN Amro Holding NV in Sydney, Greg Gibbs, director of foreign-exchange strategy would sum up the thoughts of many traders worldwide. "The conditions are revealing a new level of breakdown in the global financial system that central banks appear powerless to fix." In London, Lawrence Mutkin, head of Morgan Stanley's "European fixed income strategy" would add, "Systemic risks are extremely high, and the outlook appears bleak....term lending markets appear almost to have closed, while cash hoarding continues."[34] The seriousness of the banking crisis would be aggressively addressed by the U.S. Federal Reserve as well as central banks worldwide in an all out effort to avert a total collapse of the world financial system. No nation had foreseen the events that transpired, and the world seemed unprepared to address it, appearing to develop strategies as the crisis evolved. And, indeed, there was no reason to expect they should have anticipated the event, or have had a plan in place. So unlikely, on a statistical basis, was it for such an event to ever happen, that no nation appeared to have even remotely prepared any contingency plans relating to such an event, this is how unlikely.[35, 36, 37]

The probability of certain financial events happening over the course of time can be measured statistically as a sigma event. The higher the sigma number, the less chance of the event occurring. The chance of the premium paid by banks to one another skyrocketing upward as it did was measured as a 6.2 sigma event. Translated into English, that is to say it would take 6800 years to see such an event take place on any given day! Considered from another perspective, it would happen only on one day out of every 2,482,000![38] Yet, it all began on July 26, 2007, the week Quartet Envoy Tony Blair began his maiden trip to the Middle East to gather support for the "Promised Land" bazaar.

The initial jolt of the earthquake that shook the global financial system happened on July 26, 2007. On that day, the banking system's risk premium began its historical march skyward. But, like the physical earthquake, there was an underlying reason that ultimately led to the banking crisis. That underlying reason was a mortgage called "subprime."

Subprime mortgages made loans available to buyers of real property that, otherwise, did not meet the usual criteria for borrowing at the lowest rates that were available to the "prime" customers of banks. At first, as the new loans were made available, it appeared that someone in the lending industry had finally invented a better mouse trap. Loan applications from individuals that previously had not been able to qualify, but now could realize the American dream, began to increase. By March 2007, subprime mortgages had added up to a staggering $1.3 trillion in value on over 7.5 million homes.[39]

Although subprime loans began in America, they were sold to investors worldwide, becoming an investment vehicle for hundreds of billions of dollars for the international community. Prior to the advent of subprime loans, investing in mortgages was safe. But, by 2007, the better mouse trap began to falter, with lenders foreclosing on a staggering 1.3 million homes, most from subprime loans. By August 2008, financial firms around the world had written down their holdings of subprime-related securities by a stunning $501 billion.[40]

The Council on Foreign Relations (CFR) is perhaps the most prestigious foreign policy organization in the world with its members including many former U.S. Presidents and Secretaries of State. Its published articles are read by foreign policy makers worldwide. Perhaps because the subprime crisis was worldwide, the CFR posted a timeline of the Global Financial Meltdown on its website. It noted the Global Financial Crisis went global in August 2007, with hedge funds and banks around the world revealing large holdings of mortgage-backed securities in their portfolios.[41] Then, on August 10, 2007, central banks from around the world began a coordinated effort to inject liquidity into the credit markets for the first time since 9/11. The participants in this effort to address the beginnings of the meltdown were the central banks of the United States, Europe, Japan, Australia, and Canada. Later that August, the largest U.S. mortgage lender, Countrywide, began to indicate it had a problem, shaking the mortgage industry and making headlines nightly. On August 31, President Bush called for a bailout of U.S. homeowners unable to pay their increasing debts.[42]

From August 2007, the financial meltdown grew. In September, the British Bank Northern Rock experienced a run on its deposits with long lines forming outside its branches. Having asked the British Government for emergency funds, necessary for its survival, depositors became spooked. Eventually, the bank failed and, in February 2008, was taken over by the British Government.[43]

July through September raised the fear that a global financial meltdown was beginning. It began in July, with the failure of Indy Mac Bank, one of the largest ever to fail. In September due to rising fear that the U.S. Government would not back the trillions of dollars of mortgages supported by Fannie Mae and Freddie Mac, the world financial system hovered on the brink of collapse. On September 7, the U.S. Government nationalized both quasi-governmental entities guaranteeing their soundness. Then, six months after the failure of investment bank Bear Stearns, a series of incidents rattled the global financial markets more than anytime since the Great Depression. Bank of America stepped in to save investment bank Merrill Lynch. Shortly afterwards, the largest bankruptcy in U.S. history occurred as 150 year old Lehman Brothers investment bank failed to find a buyer. The very next day, AIG, the largest insurance company operating in the U.S. had its credit rating downgraded. But, it was able to secure a loan from the U.S. Government for $85 billion allowing it to continue operating.[45]

U.S. Secretary of the Treasury Henry Paulson, seeing that the situation could spiral out of control, unveiled a huge bank rescue plan worth $700 billion from taxpayers to stabilize the financial markets. Two days after the Paulson Plan was announced, on September 21, the remaining U.S. investment banks, Goldman Sachs and Morgan Stanley converted to bank status, ending the last of the independent investment banks on Wall Street. With their conversion, the last remaining symbols of Wall Street success during the second half of the twentieth century were gone.[46]

In an article dated September 21, 2008, *New York Post* reporter Michael Gray summed up how close the United States financial system had come to a complete meltdown, and with it the global system. He pointed out that the markets were just a few trades away from Armageddon on the previous Thursday. Gray also uncovered even more revealing information from traders inside two large custodial banks. Speaking anonymously, the traders reported that money market funds were flooded with $500 billion in sell orders just prior to the opening of trading, out of a total money-market capitalization of approximately $4 trillion! Fear was gripping traders, directly related to the seizing up of the credit markets. These same anonymous traders passed along rumors that various money market funds could be "breaking the buck," which meant the value of a dollar placed in the fund would now be worth less than a dollar.[47]

On Thursday, September 18, just prior to the market's opening, the Federal Reserve injected a whopping $105 billion stopping a potential run on cash that could have brought down large segments of the US economy. Late on that Tuesday, the Reserve Primary Fund, touted as super-safe because it only placed its investments within other institutions considered super-safe, invested in Lehman bonds. With no consideration to the notion that Lehman could default, the funds were considered completely safe. However, Lehman did default causing Reserve Primary Fund's value to drop below the all significant $1 a share level.[48]

On Wednesday, banks prepared for a potential run against their accounts. Reserves set aside for withdrawal that normally would be set at $2 billion were moved up to $90 billion. Yet, on that one day alone, $144.5 billion would be taken out of the banking system, an all time record. Just the week before, the total amount removed from money market funds was only $7.1 billion. By Thursday, the amount of withdrawals had grown to $100 billion in that one day. So far, the banking system supported by the Federal Reserve had handled the run on bank accounts, but only just barely.[49]

According to the *Post* article, a complete financial meltdown was averted by the narrowest of margins. Thankfully, September was over. Then October began and in its second week added its own mark to the history books. It was the worst point loss week in the history of the Dow Jones.[50] In November 2008, former Federal Reserve Chairman Alan Greenspan summed up the global financial meltdown as a "once in a century event."

CONCLUSION

No longer was it only the United States that was engaged in the effort to remove the "Promised Lands" from the Jewish nation. Now, for the first time a multitude of countries from across the Earth had come together in the effort, led by the Quartet group. Nations gathered together to persuade Israel that the time had finally come, in the name of peace, to relinquish the lands promised her in the ancient texts. In return, true peace was promised by her Muslim neighbors.

Earthquakes and storms usually hit only one country. Heat waves can impact an entire continent. But a financial meltdown can decimate the world. The entire world suffered during the crisis, coming terribly close to a financial abyss not visited since 1929. Only after the greatest effort on the part of the world's most prosperous and powerful nations, was disaster averted. An effort that took so many of their available financial resources, that it is reasonable to wonder if they could ever do it again should it become necessary.

The outward start of the entire "Global Financial Crisis" can be traced to July 26, 2007, with the interbank risk premium beginning its march to levels considered statistically possible once every 6,800 years, and bringing with it the international banking system to the brink of a systemic collapse. Coincidentally, the Quartet's newly appointed representative began his maiden voyage to the Middle East to gather support for the Annapolis Conference that same week.

The Conference was to be a "Promised Land" bazaar, attended by a multitude of nations from across the world. But something else about the efforts from the Quartet was even stranger than the coincidence of yet another disaster coinciding with the start of an effort to remove the "Promised Land" from the Jews.

There is another ancient Hebrew text, written by a man called Zechariah, which describes a group of four powers in the distant future. These four powers will be dedicated to removing the "Promised Land" from Israel. Like the one from Ezekiel, this text was written some 2500 years ago. When President George W. Bush organized the Quartet, consisting of the United States, European Union, United Nations and Russia, he created a group of four political powers dedicated to removing the ancient "Promised Land" from Israel. In so doing, Bush appears to have fulfilled this prophetic utterance. Based on the ancient text, the Quartet appears to have been specifically identified long ago. But, eerie as that is, it is the warning associated with the prophet's words against the four powers that carries an even more frightening message and a warning for mankind.

CHAPTER FOURTEEN

Ancient Warning of Terror

During the centuries that Jerusalem has been in existence, it has become the focal point of a multitude of peoples. Located in the beautiful Judean hills, this city is known to more people throughout history than any other. It is here that King David ruled and Solomon built his temple, and where the Jewish and Christian prophets spoke their words of events yet to happen. It also is a city associated with Jesus, where he preached and walked among the people. For Muslims, Jerusalem is where Mohammed is thought to have ascended into the sky.[1]

Over the centuries Jerusalem has been conquered many times, with various tribes and nations possessing it. But, regardless of who controlled it, the Jews retained the city as the focal point of their faith over the ages. When the Jewish people were dispersed throughout the world, they built their synagogues with the entrance always pointed toward Jerusalem. One can search throughout history for a group of people with an attachment to one city, but none compare to the Jews and Jerusalem.

There seems to be no place on Earth quite like Jerusalem. Indeed, the issues of war and peace for the entire world appear to be focused on this small piece of real estate. This is not because Jerusalem possesses any great natural wealth, nor is it located at any strategic crossroads. Yet, in the twenty-first century it remains the focal point of attention for the nations of the world.

In 1948, just prior to the Israeli declaration of independence, British forces departed from Jerusalem, which had been under their protection. Immediately after their departure, the battle between the Arabs and Jews for control of the city began in earnest. After the fighting finally ceased with the signing of the Armistice Agreements in the first half of 1949, the city was divided by a line that ran roughly north to south. Everything to the west, the New City, as well as Mount Zion, was Israeli Jerusalem. To the east, where the Western Wall is located, fell to the control of the Arabs. Under the terms of the Armistice Agreement, Jews were to have access to the Western Wall for prayer and worship, even though the Wall was located on the Arab side. But despite the truce agreement establishing that right, and the United Nations there to "enforce" its terms, the Arabs denied Jewish worshipers access. Jerusalem was a divided city. But in 1967, after the conclusion of the Six-Day War, all of Jerusalem was united under Israeli control for the first time in over 2000 years.[2, 3]

INTRACTABLE JERUSALEM

The Middle East peace effort has many thorny issues to contend with, but none even remotely approach the difficulty of Jerusalem. With both Arabs and Jews claiming it as holy, room for compromise is almost non-existent.

The Jewish connection to the city is ancient. For over 3000 years the Jews have remained consistently dedicated to the city, reciting such statements as, "Next year in Jerusalem," during the Passover service. Often they recall the city in the blessing at the end of each meal. According to a recent Jewish mayor of the city, Jerusalem represents all the Jews have prayed for and dreamed of for the last two thousand years.

When it comes to how the conflicted parties in the area see Jerusalem, a *New York Times* article in May, 2000 summed it up.

Jerusalem is rarely publicly discussed by Israeli or Palestinian leaders in anything but black-and-white terms. It is the 'eternal, undivided capital' of Israel, on the one hand, and the future capital of the Palestinian state on the other: seemingly irreconcilable concepts that have led many intelligent politicians to recommend that the issue be left unresolved in any final, peace talks[4]

Israeli law experts argue that both East Jerusalem, as well as Judea, should now be Israeli territory since Jordan did not have legal sovereignty over the territory during the time of the Six-Day War, and thus Israel was entitled in an act of self-defense to "fill the vacuum." Israel's sovereignty over West Jerusalem is a result of the similar vacuum, created when British rule ended in 1948. Israel defended itself after the Arab forces attacked, thus allowing the Jewish state to "fill the vacuum" on the west side as well. So goes the legal train of thought from the Israeli side.[5]

Jerusalem has become ingrained within Israeli legal concepts. In 1980, a foundational statute in the country's unwritten constitution was approved by the Israeli Knesset. The title of the 1980 law is, "Basic Law: Jerusalem, Capital of Israel." The law has four clauses. The first is "Jerusalem, complete and united, is the capital of Israel." Second, "Jerusalem is the seat of the President of the State, the Knesset, the Government and the Supreme Court." The third clause deals with protection of "Holy Places," and the fourth clause deals with administrative matters. Accordingly, all branches of Israeli government are seated in Jerusalem. They include the Executive or Presidential, Legislative, Judicial, and Administrative. Also, in line with this policy, the Knesset and Supreme Court buildings are located in Jerusalem.[6]

Palestinians on the other hand claim Jerusalem as the capital of a future Palestinian state, as declared in the Palestinian Declaration of Independence of 1988. In 2000, the Palestinian Authority passed a law designating East Jerusalem as its capital. The Palestinian position on Jerusalem has four key points as well, and probably not by coincidence. First, East Jerusalem is occupied territory based on United Nations Resolution 242, and it is the sovereign territory of the Palestinian state that will be established. Second, based on agreements signed with Israel, the status of Jerusalem, not just East Jerusalem, is to be part of the permanent status negotiations. Third, Jerusalem should be accessible as an open city, and remain undivided regardless of the sovereignty question. Last, it states any future Palestinian state would be committed to freedom of worship and the protection of religious sites.[7]

The United Nations has passed six Security Council Resolutions concerning the question of Israeli control of Jerusalem, declaring as invalid its attempts to unify the city. Resolution 478 declared that the 1980 Israeli "Jerusalem Law" claiming a unified Jerusalem, and annexing East Jerusalem as Israel's "eternal and indivisible" capital, was "null and void and must be rescinded forthwith." Following that resolution, U.N. member states with a presence within Jerusalem withdrew their representatives. Prior to the Resolution's passage, thirteen countries maintained their embassies in Jerusalem. Following the resolution, all thirteen moved their embassies from Jerusalem to Tel Aviv. Today, no international embassies remain in Jerusalem.[8]

The policy of the European Union is similar to that of the United Nations. Its representatives indicate that, "The EU opposes measures which would prejudge the outcome of permanent status negotiations on Jerusalem." This policy is based on the principles set out in UN Security Council Resolution 242, notably the impossibility of acquiring territory by force. The EU is concerned that Israeli policies are reducing the possibility of reaching a final status agreement on Jerusalem, and in violation of both Israel's "road map" obligations and international law.[9]

In August 2000, Brian Whitaker, Middle East editor of the *Guardian* newspaper, summed up the intractable nature of the Jerusalem issue in his, "Special Report: Israel and the Middle East." He wrote:

> Today it is the turn of King Abdullah of Jordan to meet Yasser Arafat. Yesterday it was President Mubarak of Egypt's. In the seemingly endless round of meetings, the only thing everyone agrees on is that Jerusalem has become the main stumbling block in the Middle East peace process.[10]

Jerusalem has become a negotiator's nightmare, appearing to be a knot that is impossible to untie. For Israel, it is their undivided eternal capital, with the Palestinians, it is their future capital.

THE TEMPLE MOUNT

But if a problem can have a heart, the heart of Jerusalem is the Temple Mount, also known as Mount Moriah by the Jews, and the Noble Sanctuary by Muslims. Located in a part of Jerusalem referred to as the Old City, it is the most contested religious site in the world. The Temple Mount is the Holiest site in Judaism, and the Jewish Midrash, or teachings, hold that it was from this site that the world expanded into its present form. It is also believed that God gathered dust from this place to create the first man, and according to the Jewish Torah, God chose to rest His divine presence at the Temple Mount. There have been two Jewish Temples on that site in the course of history, both destroyed in times past. But it is believed that there will be a third and final Temple built. The Temple Mount is regarded as so holy that many Jews will not set foot on it in fear of violating sacred ground. Both the Palestinian Authority and Israel claim authority over the Temple Mount area. In the 1967 war when Israeli forces took

Jerusalem, its government assigned control over the Temple Mount to the Muslim Waqf, a council of Muslim religious leaders.[11]

The Temple Mount is an area where emotions run high. In March 2005, Jordanian engineers and Palestinian laborers carved the word "Allah" on ancient stones on the "Southern Wall" enraging many Jews. Then, in 2006, a member of the Israeli Knesset announced plans for a synagogue to be built on the Mount. He pointed out that this would not replace any mosques, but correct an historical injustice and provide the Muslim Waqf an opportunity to prove its tolerance of other faiths. In 2007, a group of rabbis entered the Temple Mount, starting a firestorm of criticism. The newspaper, *Haaretz,* accused the rabbis of "knowingly and irresponsibly bringing a burning torch closer to the most flammable hill in the Middle East."[12]

There does, however, appear to be a legitimate concern as it relates to freedom of worship in the city of Jerusalem. During the nineteen years that Jordan occupied the "Jewish Quarter" of Jerusalem, all Jewish sites were destroyed, desecrated or isolated. Included in this were 68 synagogues and the ancient cemetery on the Mount of Olives, where the tombstones were removed for construction material. Israel points out that these acts were usually committed in full view of United Nations observers. Additionally, agreements providing Jewish access to holy sites were never enforced. Should the Palestinians gain control over certain areas, it is feared, they would continue the effort to destroy the Jewish holy sites. An example of Muslim disregard for Jewish holy sites is the recent destruction of Joseph's Tomb in Nablus and Shalom Al Israel synagogue in Jericho after the Palestinians were handed control.[13]

Jerusalem is the negotiator's ultimate nightmare-intractable, emotional, uncompromising, and the one impossible obstacle to a peace settlement in the most volatile dispute in the world. No city anywhere on Earth appears to possess so much significance to world peace today.

Ancient Prophecy & Terror

While the Quartet, and virtually the entire international community, came together for a "peace" settlement that would removed a portion of Jerusalem, as well as Judea from the Israelites, the ancient Hebrew Scriptures make one thing clear; nations involved in this scheme will incur the wrath of God. These actions, led by the Quartet, are a direct challenge to a promise made by God and given to the Israelites. There appears to be a very specific warning to mankind against attempting to reverse this promise from God, according to another Hebrew prophet. In this case the prophet provides details of what to look for in order to know that the time foretold is at hand.

Over the last several years the old words of this prophet appear to fit the present international effort against the modern day Israelites to an uncanny degree. Perhaps, the warning associated with his words may be unfolding as well. Many will argue that the efforts on the part of the Quartet, and world community, are dedicated to bringing peace to the region, and should not result in Divine wrath. At least on the surface it is being done in the name of peace. However, often what appears on the surface is distinctly different from reality. Regardless of the Quartet's motives, their actions run hard against the ancient promise to the Jews. Regardless of the reasoning behind the Quartet's actions, mankind ought to expect a response from his Creator if this old prophet's words are coming to life today. Indeed, it appears that response has already begun.

Sometime around the year 520 B.C., a Hebrew prophet named Zechariah reported experiencing many visions from God that revealed the future of mankind. His visions had significant apocalyptic symbolism. He mentions *The four horsemen, The two olive trees,* and *The lampstand & seven eyes.* These symbols were also mentioned in the Book of Revelations written over five centuries later by Jesus' disciple John on the Mediterranean Island of Patmos.[14]

A prophecy by Zechariah describes a time in the future when actions will be taken to remove part of the "Promised Land" from the Israelites. The prophecy eerily describes events currently unfolding as it relates to the Quartet's efforts. We pick up from the Book of Zechariah Chapter 1.

> *Then lifted I up mine eyes, and saw, and behold four horns. And I said unto the angel that talked with me, What be these? And he answered me, These are the horns which have scattered Judah, Israel, and Jerusalem.*[15]

In the vision he describes a scene of *four horns,* and wondering what they are he asks the angel, *What are these?* The answer comes that the *four horns* are engaged in an effort that ultimately scatters Judah, Israel, and Jerusalem. The Quartet is comprised of four distinct governmental entities, the United States, Russia, European Union, and the United Nations. The Quartet powers have gathered the nations of the world together to scatter the land of Judah, what is today often called the West Bank, and Jerusalem. But, in spite of the world community's involvement, there is little doubt that the main players are the Quartet. According to the old Hebrew Scriptures, this is a direct challenge to God whose promise to the Israelites from long ago is being challenged today, just as a similar promise was challenged some 3500 years ago by Egypt. In this case, it is not one nation involved in the challenge, but four powers and they have now gathered the world behind their efforts. As we saw in the previous chapter, this effort on the part of the Quartet began in earnest on July 23, 2007. But if there is any question as to what exactly the horns in the vision represent, we don't have to guess, it is given to us in this next passage along with more information.

> *And the LORD shewed me four carpenters. Then said I, What come these to do? And he spake, saying, These are the horns which have scattered Judah, so that no man did lift up his head: but*

these are come to fray them, to cast out the <u>horns of the Gentiles,</u>
which lifted up their horn over the land of Judah to scatter it.[16]
(underline added)

Over 2500 years ago these Hebrew writings indicated that, at a time in the future, a group of four political powers will unite in an effort to *scatter* the lands of Judah, Israel, and Jerusalem. We are further told that God will send *carpenters* to do something that will *fray (to make afraid) the* powers who are attempting to reverse His promise to the Israelites. Obviously, this prophecy could not have been fulfilled until the restoration of Israel in 1948. We do not know exactly what terrifying events the *carpenters* will produce, but here, too, we see another interesting coincidence.

During the time the Quartet restarted its scheme to *scatter* the lands of Judea, the world was terrified by an extremely unusual event; the most severe world financial system meltdown since 1929. For the first time since that infamous year, individuals and institutions essentially pulled out of a financial system that until only recently was viewed as completely secure. That fear, or terror, of a collapsing financial system has been a great concern on the minds of many with governments making great efforts to stop it. But, as hundreds of billions of dollars were being removed from the "safest" financial instruments in the world, and sent to the proverbial mattress, this action appears to be the truest measure of the sentiment toward the "Global Financial Meltdown." It is, therefore, reasonable to conclude that the global community has experienced a common event that has terrified them, qualifying as a possible act of the *carpenters*.

In this ancient Hebrew Scripture we see a clear warning issued to any and all nations that attempt to *scatter* the lands of Judah. It points to four powers that unite in the effort and says that they will suffer for their actions against God's will. Those *four horns* appear to be the Quartet, with perhaps the first of the four *carpenters* appearing on April 30,

2003, at the Quartet's first gathering. As covered in Chapters 10 and 11, that first Quartet conference was met with the worst weather in U.S. history, immediately followed by the worst heat wave in the last 250 years of European history. The global financial meltdown might represent the 2nd of the four *carpenters*.

It is true that two of the four political entities that make up the Quartet are the European Union as well as the United Nations. One might argue that these do not really represent nation states, per se, and thus do not qualify as two of Zechariah's *horns*. However, upon analysis, both do qualify. Consider this. Both the European Union and United Nations have a constitution. They both have a city considered their seat of government. Each has a flag and a foreign policy representative to the nations of the world. Both have a political leader and a legislature made up of members from various states, not unlike the Congress of the United States. As in the case of the United States, those member states still retain their government offices and identity even though they are a part of the United States. In that sense, both the European Union and United Nations qualify as nations, from the standpoint of Zachariah's words.

But Zechariah had more to say, describing another event that coincides with our current day. He goes on to talk about how difficult it will become for the nations of the world to deal with Jerusalem, perfectly describing current circumstances relating to that city. This, from Chapter 12 of the Book named after him.

> *Behold, I will make Jerusalem a cup of trembling unto all the people round about, when they shall be in the siege both against Judah and against Jerusalem. And in that day will I make Jerusalem a burdensome stone for all people: all that burden themselves with it shall be cut in pieces, though all the people of the earth be gathered together against it.* [17]

This passage is disquieting in how closely it echoes the current Middle East "peace" process. The Quartet, and now almost the entire International community, is asking Israel to give up Judah, and a portion of Jerusalem, to form a nation to be called Palestine. This is described in the prophetic passage as a *siege both against Judah and Jerusalem*. Virtually the entirety of this "peace" effort on the part of the world is designed to pressure Israel on this point. This prophetic passage points out that the *people of the earth be gathered against* Judah and Jerusalem. The peoples of the Earth have indeed gathered against Judah and Jerusalem, beginning with the Annapolis Conference. In fact, the Annapolis Conference constituted a gathering of over 45 nations and international organizations from across the globe for the expressed purpose of *scattering* the land of Judah from the Israelites in the name of peace.

The gathering of nations at Annapolis also sought to accomplish the division of Jerusalem. The passage warns that the City of Jerusalem will cause itself to become a great *burdensome stone for all peoples* and that *all that burden themselves with it shall be torn to pieces*. The old Hebrew writings indicate that when Judah is under siege, Jerusalem will become a *cup of trembling* for the nations of the world. Indeed, intractable Jerusalem has become just that. Yet another warning is issued to mankind concerning Jerusalem, that all nations joining the effort to remove it from the possession of the Jews *shall be torn to pieces*.

So as the world sets forth to *scatter* the land of Judah, it runs directly into the headwinds of ancient Hebrew warnings that long ago foretold this very action. It is an action that is completely in contradiction to a promise from God, that these lands would be restored to a re-born nation of Israel.

As mankind attempts to reverse this ancient promise, he has faced the great difficulties foretold in these old writings. Now, the real question relates to the future. What should mankind expect if he actually succeeds in his attempts to *scatter* Judah? According to these ancient warnings, he should expect to be *torn to pieces,* the details of which are left to the imagination of the reader. It should be expected that God would, at some point in time, restore the lands back to Israel keeping His promise true. In fact, the efforts to *scatter* Judah have already resulted in numerous Israeli settlements being *scattered* from the possession of the Jews. What is called progress toward a "comprehensive peace settlement" by the Quartet, and the international community they now lead, is referred to in the ancient Hebrew Scriptures as a *scattering* of the land of Judah, with Divine wrath promised.

As the Middle East "peace" effort moves forward it will, no doubt, continue to focus attention on the establishment of a Palestinian state on the land of Judea and Samaria. Based on reports from the negotiations, it is clear that East Jerusalem is to be the capital of this newly formed state of Palestine. Zechariah refers to the effort to *scatter* the land in the past tense, indicating that it will take place. Consider the passage *These are the horns which have scattered Judah, Israel, and Jerusalem.* The prophet is pointing out that in his vision, the land of Judah, Israel, and Jerusalem was, in fact, *scattered.* This tells us that the efforts of the Quartet and the international community will eventually succeed in their goal of a comprehensive "peace" agreement between Israel and the Palestinian/Arab community.

However, according to this Scripture, one should be careful what he wishes for, because he may get it. Having succeeded in the effort to obtain a treaty by trading Judah and Jerusalem, the ancient Hebrew Scriptures warn that the world will experience the *four carpenters* that *are come to fray them.* It appears that two such events have taken place since the Quartet (*four horns*) began their efforts in 2003. If this passage is implying that a total of four events will be visited upon those *scattering* the land, then it leaves two more events of terror remaining.

RICE'S STATEMENT

In December 2008, the Quartet and nations of the world appeared to be moving closer to dividing the land. Secretary of State Rice's statement on the status of the Quartet's efforts for a Middle East "peace" agreement was recorded in the *Jerusalem Post* at that time:[18]

> Rice spoke to reporters after a meeting of the diplomatic Quartet of Mideast peacemakers, the US, the UN, the European Union and Russia, which said the Israeli-Palestinian negotiating process launched by Bush at Annapolis, Maryland is 'irreversible' and should be intensified to 'establish as soon as possible the state of Palestine.

Rice went on to describe the "progress" that was made as a result of the Annapolis Conference:

> This is the first time in almost a decade that Palestinians and Israelis are addressing all of the core issues in a comprehensive way to try to get to a solution, and if that process takes a little bit longer, so be it,' she said. 'But we are very much further along, certainly than we were in 2001, and I would argue even than in 2007 when Annapolis was concluded.

Rice went on to describe the role of the world community in the effort, as if taking a paragraph from the ancient writings:

> The council was scheduled to...adopt the resolution, which US officials said has very wide support. I believe that will then add the voice of the international community, through its most powerful and its most consequential body, that is the Security Council, to establish...the Annapolis process as the way forward.

Proudly, Rice had announced the effort, led by the Quartet, to divide Judah and Jerusalem from Israel, pointing out the "wide support" across the globe and within the Security Council. However, no longer was the effort confined to the auspices of the United Nations. Now, a multitude of individual nations met at Annapolis in support of the Quartet's cause. But, in talking about the involvement of this multitude of nations, Secretary Rice might have said, *all the people of the earth be gathered together against it.*

CHAPTER FIFTEEN

The Israel Omen

Perhaps, having not seen God's supernatural intervention on behalf of the Jews for many ages, mankind has relegated such notions to the status of legends and myths, something not to be calculated in this modern day. Some might say that it doesn't really matter if those prophecies were given long ago and recently fulfilled, the world view they embrace does not allow for a God that would intervene in such a way. Or, perhaps, some will believe that such things happened in olden times, but of course, not today. Whatever the explanations of the phenomena of continuous coincidences since 1991, one thing is certain. The nation of Israel is back in the "Promised Land" just as in ancient times, and until recently those words had not been spoken for over two thousand years.

The journey back to this land was not an easy one. As recently as the early 1940s, the Jews suffered methodical attempts of extermination by one of history's most fanatical Jew haters, Adolph Hitler. But what Hitler did not know as he hunkered down in his bunker in 1945, was that his efforts to eliminate the people he so hated, would ultimately build the case for the rebirth of the nation they so longed for. With the United Nations vote in 1947 to establish the Jewish state, that international body was unwittingly fulfilling the ancient Hebrew prophecies. The nation's birth, in spite of the best efforts of numerous Arab nations and their armies to prevent it, made it even more impressive.

The ancient words of the prophet Ezekiel, spoken over 2500 years ago, echo in the lands now possessed by the ones of whom he spoke. This man was so prolific as a prophet, that he even left us a mathematical formula for calculating the year in which his prophecy of the Jews' return as the nation of Israel, after being *scattered among the heathen,* would take place. In "The Valley of Dry Bones," Ezekiel takes the reader on a journey of the impossible, where the chance of rebirth is described in terms that are uniquely improbable. Yet, he did not stop there. Instead, he goes on to describe some of the characteristics that would be present during their rebirth in the distant future.

Instead of the rebirth involving both ancient Jewish states, Israel and Judah, it would involve only one, Israel. In chapter 37 of the Book of Ezekiel, *and I will make them one nation in the land...they shall no longer be two nations...* He goes on as well to describe the transformation of the land from its destitute condition of the early 20th century, to the flower of the Middle East that it is today.

The wars of 1948 and 1967 secured lands from enemies that chose to use them as launching pads to strike an otherwise peaceful nation. Ironically, those attacking Israel caused even more of the ancient "Promised Land," spoken of by Ezekiel, to be acquired. The peace efforts that today center on negotiating away much of these "Promised Lands," will ultimately place Israel in a life-threatening position, vulnerable to the numerous Arab neighbors whose religious beliefs prevent them from living in peace with a Jewish state.

The first President Bush's efforts in October 1991 were sincere, as peace is a noble goal. But the ultimate aim of the effort in Madrid was to implement two United Nations resolutions that explicitly required the land to be removed from the possession of the Jews, something that would effectively reverse a promise of God. On the very same day that the conference opened, a powerful "freak of nature," three storms combining into one reached the zenith of its might as it slammed into the New England coast, even damaging the President's home there. This "Perfect Storm," as it was christened, eventually became a Hollywood movie. Not many storms have that distinction, nor do they possess 100' high waves. This marked the beginning of the Madrid effort.

But Madrid continued without any "progress" until the elevation of Yitzhak Rabin to the office of Prime Minister of Israel. As a P.M. that embraced the idea of "land for peace," he was a welcome change to a Washington administration whose policy had lined up with the United Nations Resolutions requiring the ancient "Promised Land" to be removed from Israel. The day the sixth round of the Madrid Conference began in Washington, August 24, 1992, Rabin would be there. On that very same day in southern Florida, the fourth most powerful hurricane in U.S. history would strike, becoming the most costly natural disaster in U.S. history, up to that time.

The next year would see the "land for peace" efforts score their first big success, culminating in a peace accord between the Palestinians and Israel that was signed on the White House lawn in September 1993. Negotiations between the Israelis and Palestinians started in April of that year, with an agreement finalized by August. Interestingly, the entire time the Rabin government was negotiating an agreement of land for peace at the urging of the United States, nine Midwestern states experienced the "Great Flood," which the National Weather Service described as "one of the most significant and damaging natural disasters ever to hit the United States." It was a flood not seen for 500 years!

After that accord between the Palestinians and Israelis, the Clinton administration sought to take advantage of an opening with Assad of

Syria in his dispute with Israel. On January 16, 1994, the President met with Assad in Geneva, Switzerland to discuss land for peace. So fruitful were these talks, two days later, on January 18, Prime Minister Rabin announced that Israeli citizens should be prepared to give up the land of the Golan Heights. Yet, the day between the Clinton-Assad meeting and Rabin's announcement, the United States suffered the highest ever instrumentally recorded earthquake in an urban area. The Northridge quake was so damaging that only Hurricane Andrew exceeded its cost at that time.

In 2001, the new Bush Administration began its foreign policy approach in the Middle East conflict by allowing the parties to try to work it out themselves. But, by mid-2001, it decided to become more involved and announced on June 5 CIA Director George Tenet would visit the region to help promote the Mitchell Committee's report. The essence of the report was that Israel needed to stop settling the lands in dispute, otherwise called the "Promised Land." This represented a significant shift in the new administration's approach. On the same day Tenet's trip was announced, the National Weather Service observed a storm off the Texas coast that "went right from nothing to a tropical storm!" The storm would dump an enormous amount of rainfall over the Houston area, only to return to do it again with such massive flooding that the Houston Chronicle would christen it the "Great Flood of 2001," with that tropical storm considered the worst ever.

Later in that same year, President Bush would have to placate a very angry and alienated Saudi Arabia, delivering to them what no other American president had ever agreed to. What the Bush Administration offered in its efforts to make amends with the Saudis was an historic shift in U.S. Middle East policy: support for the establishment of a Palestinian state in ancient Judea and Samaria. This shift was as strong a challenge to the ancient promises from God recorded in the old Hebrew texts as could be made. With much fanfare, the new policy was to be announced during the week of September 10, 2001.

Slightly more than a year and a half later, the Middle East group of four called the "Quartet" launched its long awaited "road map" peace plan to establish a Palestinian state by 2005. The Quartet, led by the United States with the European Union playing a significant role, began the conference on April 30, 2003. That very same day marked the beginning of the most severe weather in United States history, with 562 tornadoes, 1,587 hail storms, and 740 reports of wind damage. But Mother Nature wasn't finished yet. When the rash of tornados finally ended in the United States, a heat wave began in Europe, the other main "road map" participant. That heat wave was considered the worst in over 250 years with the death toll from that tragic event reaching a staggering 50,000 lives. This event possibly represented one of the actions of the Biblical *carpenters* warned of.

But, the diligent efforts of those promoting "land for peace" finally paid dividends in August 2005 with the Israeli withdrawal from Gaza and several settlements in Judea and Samaria, better known today as the West Bank. That forced evacuation from the "Promised Land" officially ended on August 23, 2005. On that same day, tropical depression No. Twelve was identified by the National Hurricane Center for the first time. It was soon to be named tropical storm Katrina, destined to live in infamy.

After the "success" of seeing the Israelis leave Gaza, and several West Bank settlements, there was a lull in the "peace" efforts. Then, in late July 2007, the Quartet's representative, Tony Blair, began diplomacy that would ultimately result in the Annapolis Middle East Peace Conference to be held that November. In attendance would be 45 nations and world organizations. Finally, the effort to promote a peace treaty centering on the concept of "land for peace" had gone global. Never before had so many nations, from every corner of the globe, gathered to pressure the

Israelites for a reversal of a promise from God Himself, according to ancient Hebrew Scriptures.

With the participation of the global community, substantial progress would be made toward a "comprehensive peace settlement." The agreement's essential component would remove large parts of the "Promised Land" from Israel. This potentially watershed development in the dispute began on July 23, 2007 as Blair began his first trip to the Middle East to gain support for the Annapolis Conference. The conference succeeded in establishing a framework for the Israelis and Palestinians to work on over the course of the next year, making historic progress in the land for peace process. But, the exact week the effort began on the diplomatic front, the beginnings of a financial earthquake started with an historical move in banking fear that would soon bring the world banking system to the brink of collapse. This near-collapse appears to represent the second of the "carpenters" warned of in the old writings.

Perhaps, the time has come to consider whether mankind's "land for peace" effort in the Middle East dispute might be crossing some prophetic, Godly line that he should not violate. If the events since 1991 represent a warning against reversing a promise by God, then they also constitute an omen for the future. This Israel omen of natural, and not-so-natural, disasters coinciding with negotiations to remove the "Promised Land," may portend a dramatically more devastating event in the future. Especially, as the "land for peace" process moves forward with the powerful Quartet leading the charge. What such an event would be is open to speculation. But, considering the uniquely destructive nature of each of the events since 1991, it does not bode well.

Since Zechariah's prophecies have so far come to pass, we should then believe that the efforts to trade the "Promised Land" for a peace treaty will eventually succeed. This "success" will, however, come about from the efforts and united actions of four powers, which is where the

Quartet appears to come into play. We are also told these efforts will re-sult in the unleashing of *four carpenters* that promise to terrorize a world that has crossed God. Whether or not this particular part of Zechariah's ancient prophecies has begun to unfold is also open to speculation. But, what we do know is that the effort to divide the "Promised Land" is now led by *four horns,* powers that have rallied the world in their cause, which was also predicted by Zechariah.

As the Quartet began its effort in 2003, weather in both the United States and Europe went off the charts. Then four years later, in July 2007, a great crack opened in the global financial system, just as the next Quartet effort began. Perhaps this is purely a coincidence. That too is open for speculation. But this coincidence, against the backdrop of the old prophetic words, is uncanny to say the least. If, however, it is not a coincidence, then it is possible that the four Biblical *carpenters* represent a total of four terrible events, leaving two more events to follow in the years ahead, probably on a comparable scale to the financial meltdown.

As mankind moves forward to establish a Palestinian state on lands the ancient Hebrew Scriptures say is given to Israel, is this, perhaps, a challenge to God Himself? Do some or even all of the events represent a message being sent to mankind by nature, a warning perhaps that his actions are running hard against a promise of the Creator? A case can be made that eight of the ten events looked at in these pages are significant to the day, or week, relative to a land for peace effort that was being made. But, it is not only the timing relative to the ten events that should be considered.

Although we know there are always storms, tornados, floods and earthquakes taking place, it is significant that these whose timing is as-sociated with the "land for peace" process have been historical in nature. If Hurricane Andrew is the fourth strongest storm in U.S. history, then it means almost all before it were not as severe. If a storm is described as a "once in a hundred year" freak of nature, even christened the "Perfect Storm," it was unusual to say the least. If an earthquake is the strongest ever to strike in an urban area, and causes the second most financial damage in U.S. history, that says much. If American soil suffers a severe attack for the first time since Pearl Harbor, that is a rare event. If a tropical storm instantly develops off the coast, then proceeds to generate what will be described as the Great Flood, and doubles back to do it again, it is long remembered in the area as an oddity. If 562 tornados strike over a course of days in what is described as the worst weather in U.S. history, immediately followed by the worst European heat wave in 250 years, what is there to compare them to?

Then there is Katrina, the most destructive storm in U.S. history. What more need be said? Therefore, it is not only the uncanny timing of these events, such as the global financial meltdown, but their highly unusual, even historic severity that lends itself to the speculation within these pages.

In January 2009 Israel aroused the anger of the world for its incursion into Gaza to put an end the thousands of rockets that had been raining down upon its southern cities since the Palestinians were given control over the area in August 2005. The increasing range and destructiveness of these weapons appeared to have become a true national security issue for the Jewish nation. The largest Israeli cities coming within range of these rocket attacks are Ashkelon and Ashdod, both with populations over 120,000. But, even here, we see ancient Hebrew words coming to life.

The prophet Zephaniah in the 600s B.C. foretold a day, in the distant future, where *Gaza would be forsaken, and Ashkelon a desolation; they shall drive out Ashdod at the noon day.* Gaza was indeed *forsaken* in August 2005 with the Israeli withdrawal that was supposed to bring peace there. Exactly who *they* are that will *drive out Ashdod at the noon day,* perhaps citizens fleeing to air raid shelters from rocket attacks, we are not told.

However, the militants of the Palestinian group Hamas appear to be an excellent candidate to fulfill those ancient words. To make *Ashkelon a desolation* would only take a tipping of the Palestinian rockets with a more lethal substance, which is not difficult to foresee. But Zephaniah's words could not have been fulfilled for over two thousand years, since the Jews have only recently come back into the land, and even more recently *forsaken* Gaza. So today we see another coincidence associated with the ancient words, at a time when the Quartet's efforts appear to be fulfilling the words of another prophet, Zechariah. Today, with *four horns* making headway in removing the "Promised Land" from Israel, his words also have finally come to life.

As mankind ignores prophetic signs unfolding within his midst, he does so from a lack of belief in such things having any significance to his affairs. Thus, he does not delve into these matters any longer, relegating them to an age long past, and without value. But, in so doing he potentially misses an important omen of danger that draws near. Perhaps, mankind's modernity has blinded him to significant information directly relating to his future, because it comes from an ancient source. However, that information from a prophetic standpoint appears to well describe events unfolding today, even in detail. If this is the case, then the ancient words are now screaming out to be heard.

CHAPTER SIXTEEN

The Next Catastrophe

I f, indeed, the world has been experiencing some kind of quid pro quo of disasters relative to political efforts that violate an ancient Divine promise, then the real question is this: will the phenomena continue to take place in the future, and if so, what should we now be looking for? If there is merit to the position presented in these pages, then in the years ahead there should be a continuation of these "coincidences." However, if "coincidences" simply cease, even as grand gatherings take place whose main goal is to remove the "Promised Land" from the Jews, the entire point made within these pages should rightfully be called into question. However, in the event they do continue, or even intensify, then the warning they represent to mankind should become obvious, even to the skeptic. With this in mind, it is time to consider what to look for in the months and years ahead.

THE POLITICAL-CATASTROPHE-MATRIX

Prior to 1991, the United States made no substantial efforts to remove any part of the fabled "Promised Land" from Israel. It is true that the Sinai

Peninsula, taken in the 1967 Six-Day War, had returned to Egypt after the 1979 peace treaty negotiated by Jimmy Carter. But that land was not included within the ancient borders described by Ezekiel, and there appeared no catastrophe associated with its return. However, starting in 1991, diplomacy on the part of the United States pursued a peace agreement in large part by removing segments of the land promised. This diplomatic effort began with the first Madrid Conference representing a significant breakthrough at that time. That conference would, therefore, mark the beginning of efforts on the part of the U.S. government to remove the lands promised in the ancient writings, and more ominously, the beginning of the ten historic catastrophes coinciding with those efforts in the years that followed. Looking back at the political efforts preceding the ten catastrophes, it may be possible to construct a kind of, "political-catastrophe-matrix," which when applied to future political events should signal if we can expect a catastrophe of some type as well. Here is the structure for such a matrix, based on the ten historical disasters.

In constructing the matrix, the ten events will be broken down into 3 basic types. The first type pertains to catastrophes associated with a **significant first effort** on the part of a U.S. President, with the ultimate goal being the removal of a part of the "Promised Land." There have been three U.S. Presidents since 1991: George H.W. Bush, William Jefferson Clinton, and George W. Bush. For George H.W. Bush, the "breakthrough" Madrid Peace Conference saw the Perfect Storm strike on the same day. That conference marked his administration's first significant Middle East peace effort. **CLASSIFIED: Significant First Effort**

The first effort from the Clinton Administration was the historical agreement ultimately signed on the White House lawn in September 1993. It was negotiated from April-August of that year, with the "worst natural disaster in U.S. history" unfolding month-by-month alongside the negotiations. **CLASSIFIED: Significant First Effort**

The administration of George W. Bush would come to power in

January 2001, bringing with it an initial intention of not engaging the Middle East peace process unless the parties themselves became more amenable to an agreement. This abruptly changed on June 5th, when the administration announced that CIA Director Tenet would go to the region. Just as abruptly, on the same day his mission was announced Texas experienced a storm that "...went right from nothing to a tropical storm!" suddenly appearing in the Gulf of Mexico, and causing historical flooding to the President's home state. It would be christened by the *Houston Chronicle* as the "Great Flood," with the storm's name retired.

This particular Middle East mission by CIA Director Tenet was *not* a significant effort on the part of the new Bush Administration, at least when compared to the first efforts of the previous two administrations. For George H.W. Bush, his first was an historical conference, and for Clinton, an historical agreement. George W. Bush's significant first effort would come later in 2001, when the President would try to soothe the angry Saudis, taking a step that no other American president had been willing to take in announcing U.S. support for the establishment of a Palestinian state in the middle of the "Promised Land." This watershed move, designed to placate the largest exporter of oil to the United States, was set to be announced the week of September 10, 2001, and represented a significant first effort for Bush and the "land for peace" crowd.

CLASSIFIED: Significant First Effort

There appears to be two other types of political actions that preceded the other six catastrophes. They were efforts that brought some form of **significant new success**, and/or the appearance of a new international group indicating a **significant new effort**. Consider the following examples from the remaining six events.

After President George H.W. Bush's foray with the initial Madrid Conference, peace talks were held several times in the ensuing months, but without any catastrophes matching the meetings. There was, however, no Prime Minister on the Israeli side allowing the talks to progress any further, that was until the 6th round held in Washington on August 24, 1992. With an agreeable Israeli Prime Minister finally participating for the first time, significant progress would be made eventually leading to a historical agreement the next year. On the day that conference opened, Hurricane Andrew devastated South Florida. President Bush would soon lose the Presidential election and his efforts toward the Middle East would end. **CLASSIFIED: Significant New Success**

President Clinton, after the initial success of the historic agreement between the Israelis and Palestinians signed in September 1993, would turn his attention toward Syria in January 1994. As his next big effort, Clinton would seek a peace settlement with Syria by removing the Golan Heights from Israel. He found such a degree of success after meeting with the Syrian leader, that the Israeli Prime Minister, Rabin, announced to the Israeli public the need to return that portion of the "Promised Land." That significant success was met by the Northridge, California earthquake. Clinton would see no more significant *new* success for the remainder of his administration, experiencing one frustrating failure after another. **CLASSIFIED: Significant New Success**

Then, in 2003, the long awaited "road map" peace conference presented by the newly formed International group called the Quartet met in the United States, its goal to establish a Palestinian state on the "Promised Land" by 2005. This effort, the brain child of the Bush Administration, would represent a gathering of the strongest political and financial forces in the world for the purpose of trading land for peace. It began on April 30, 2003, along with the "worst weather in U.S. history." When that catastrophe ended in the United States, it was quickly followed by the worst heat wave in the last 250 years in Europe, the other significant participant in the conference. **CLASSIFIED: Significant New Effort**

President Bush's continuing efforts to remove the ancient lands from the Israelis, in the belief it would lead to a peace agreement, finally paid off in August of 2005 with the withdrawal of Israeli forces from Gaza and several West Bank towns. But on the day of the official conclusion of the removal of Jews from the land promised, Katrina would first be noticed as a tropical depression, soon to remove hundreds of thousands of Americans from their homes. It would also mark the beginning of the end for Bush's effectiveness and popularity as President. On the Israeli side, Sharon would suffer a massive stroke in less than four months, removing him from the powerful office he held. **CLASSIFIED: Significant New Success**

Finally, in July 2007, the world rallied for the Annapolis Peace Conference, representing a first for the "land for peace" effort by bringing together over 45 nations in the effort to remove the "Promised Land." Within three days of that group's envoy, Tony Blair's, first meetings in the Middle East aimed at bringing about Annapolis, the banking system would start an event statistically expected once every 6,800 years, ultimately bringing the world financial system to the brink of collapse. **CLASSIFIED: Significant New Effort**

THE DIFFERENCE AN ELECTION CAN MAKE

The election of Yitzhak Rabin in 1992, replacing the skeptical Shamir brought dramatic changes to the Israeli negotiating approach at the peace talks, pleasing then President Bush and his Secretary of State. Rabin's election was destined to usher in an historical agreement that was impossible to foresee before he became Israel's Prime Minister. He would continue on that course until an assassin's bullet ended his life in November 1995. In America, it would take the election of George W. Bush in 2000 to bring a declaration of support for the establishment of a Palestinian state, directly in the middle of the "Promised Land." That single act represented something no previous American President had ever been willing to do. But the Presidential fate of George W. Bush would begin unraveling in a long and historic slide immediately after Hurricane Katrina, which began immediately after he and Israeli Prime Minister Sharon succeeded in removing a portion of the ancient land from Israel.

The election of Barack Obama may be a similar kind of election, one destined to alter the Middle East equation yet again. As of August 2009, it is still too early to tell. It is generally understood that he will, at a minimum, continue the direction of his predecessor in calling for the establishment of a Palestinian state on the "Promised Lands."[1]

However, as the Obama Administration was settling in at the White House, a new leader was taking the reins of power on the other side of the world. The electorate of Israel, having soured to the notion that land can buy peace, elected Benjamin Netanyahu, leader of the conservative Likud party. Having seen the results of efforts to buy peace through land transfers, the voters of Israel shifted to the right, at least as it pertains to giving up land. One of the main reasons for the shift was Gaza. After Israel unilaterally withdrew from the highly contentious area, the Palestinians chose to use their new independence to dramatically increase rocket attacks against Israeli civilian targets, eventually necessitating Israeli military action to destroy their bases. Additionally, the Gaza Palestinians would forge an alliance with Iran and its fanatical leader, who promised another Holocaust for the Jews, this time nuclear.

With Obama seeking an historical Middle East agreement, and Netanyahu seeing the reality that land transfers have produced less peace, not more, the likelihood of the two coming together for a breakthrough appears remote at best. So what should we expect in the months and years ahead that could result in a test of the "Political-Catastrophe-Matrix?"

THE NEXT CATASTROPHE

Using the "Matrix," the next catastrophe should take place when the Obama Administration, probably under the auspices of the Quartet, makes a significant first effort that would ultimately remove a portion of the land. The first effort should break new ground, probably marked by some grand gathering of the Quartet. Another "Matrix" action could be a major shift in U.S. policy against Israel, and her possession of the "Promised Land," or something akin to George W. Bush's watershed announcement in support of a Palestinian state.

It is clear from recent statements that Obama is placing his faith in the "road map" peace process, initiated by the Quartet in 2003. This appears to indicate that the *four horns,* spoken of in the ancient writings of Zechariah, will continue for a while longer in their effort to divide the land. Those old utterances promised terror against the nations seeking to remove the "Promised Land," and foretold *four carpenters* that would bring the promised terror. It now appears that two such events have already taken place. Those events, the 2003 "worst weather in U.S. history," immediately followed by the worst European heat wave in 250 years; and the global financial meltdown.

These catastrophes match all too well with the ancient warning. So perhaps it is the actions of the Quartet and their "road map" process that needs to be watched in the months and years ahead. Based on the political-catastrophe-matrix, a breakthrough gathering of this group should produce a catastrophe on a scale that rivals the financial meltdown, or frighteningly, even worse. Should that happen and the catastrophe can once again be linked to their effort, mankind would do well to begin listening to the ancient words.

On July 11, 2009, in a speech noticed by few observers, Javier Solana, a key "Quartet" figure representing the European Union, indicated that the international community may have to impose a solution on Israel. Interpretation: Israel will be forced by the international community to relinquish the "Promised Land," with the effort led by this group of four. This statement appears to be a harbinger of what the next several years will hold for Israel, and the restored "Promised Land," as the *four horns* forcefully attempt to reverse the ancient promise. Should this be the intent of the Quartet, they would do well to consider the ancient words before proceeding.

TO THE LOGICAL MIND

The litany of events catalogued within
The Israel Omen testifies to the supernatural nature of
the Bible. And if supernatural, then it is a message from
the Divine. If a message from the Divine, then it is of
the greatest importance to the individual. Therefore,
since it directs the individual to the Son of God
as their only eternal hope, then...

APPENDIX A

The Promised Land

It is believed by the Jews that God specifically promised them certain lands for their Jewish nation, as described in the ancient Hebrew Scriptures. These lands are referred to as the "Promised Land" of Israel. In addition to that promise, it appears that the re-establishment of Israel the nation, after over 2000 years of being *scattered among the heathens* of the world, was predicted in these same writings, and has added its voice to the promises of God to the Jews. This prediction and the promise to the Jews returns us to our original question: If mankind attempts to reverse these promises, what would the consequences be? Would this modern age experience something like the ten plagues ancient Egypt experienced long ago? Would it be a response on the part of nature against those that would dare try to reverse the Creator's will? As we look at the various promises recorded in the Hebrew Scriptures, let's keep an eye on the purpose for doing so. Then as we review ten major disasters that have taken place during attempts to remove this land, a pattern begins to form.

To appreciate the significance of the "Promised Land" as it relates to the Jews, and to understand the Biblical warnings to outside nations against meddling with this land, we must go back to the very beginning of the Jewish Nation, some 3,500 years ago.[1] Although its people were scattered *among the heathens* for the last 2000 years, Israel became a country again in 1948.

It is a place where only a few dim lamps light our way down the paths of recorded history. The story begins with a man who is considered the founding patriarch of Judaism, Christianity, and Islam: Abram of Ur, a resident of ancient Mesopotamia who lived some 3800 years ago. In Abram's day, Mesopotamia was an advanced society by the standards of that time. Many Mesopotamians could read and write and there were craftsmen of many skills as well as an elite religious structure. But one of the things that Abram would not accept from his society was the notion of many gods, polytheism, even though it was generally accepted by the people of that time. Instead, Abram embraced the idea that there was but one God who was in control of-and the source of-all existence, and it was He that Abram chose to follow.[2]

When Abram accepted the radical belief in one God, the ancient Hebrew Scriptures indicate that God appeared to him to confirm his convictions. At that point God changed Abram's name to Abraham and told him to depart from the land of his fathers. God send him on his first trip to the future land of Israel, the land known as Canaan. Here is the initial record of this interaction between God and Abraham. Genesis chapter 12:

> *Now the LORD had said unto Abram, Get thee out of thy country, and from thy kindred, and from thy father's house, unto a land that I will shew thee: And I will make of thee a great nation, and I will bless thee, and make thy name great; and thou shalt be a blessing... And Abram took Sarai his wife... and they went forth to go into the land of Canaan; and into the land of Canaan they came...And the LORD appeared unto Abram, and said, Unto thy seed will I give this land...[3]*

So great was Abraham's faith in his God, that he left all he had known and departed for a strange land when God gave him those words. Abraham simply left on a journey, for where, he did not know. He trusted that the God he worshiped would reveal to him this "Promised Land" when He was ready to do so.

THE PROMISED LAND

The "Promised Land," to which the Jews returned as a nation again in 1948, is described in the Book of Ezekiel, chapter 47:13-20. It includes the whole modern lands of Lebanon, the West Bank, Gaza Strip, and a small part of Syria called the Golan Heights. The side of the border next to Egypt ends at the River of Egypt, which many contemporary scholars believe refers to a river that is just within the Negev desert, near El-Arish.

¹³Thus saith the Lord GOD; This shall be the border, whereby ye shall inherit the land according to the twelve tribes of Israel: Joseph shall have two portions.

¹⁴And ye shall inherit it, one as well as another: concerning the which I lifted up mine hand to give it unto your fathers: and this land shall fall unto you for inheritance.

¹⁵And this shall be the border of the land toward the north side, from the great sea, the way of Hethlon, as men go to Zedad;

¹⁶Hamath, Berothah, Sibraim, which is between the border of Damascus and the border of Hamath; Hazarhatticon, which is by the coast of Hauran.

¹⁷And the border from the sea shall be Hazarenan, the border of Damascus, and the north northward, and the border of Hamath. And this is the north side.

¹⁸And the east side ye shall measure from Hauran, and from Damascus, and from Gilead, and from the land of Israel by Jordan, from the border unto the east sea. And this is the east side.

¹⁹And the south side southward, from Tamar even to the waters of strife in Kadesh, the river to the great sea. And this is the south side southward.

²⁰The west side also shall be the great sea from the border, till a man come over against Hamath. This is the west side.

²¹So shall ye divide this land unto you according to the tribes of Israel.

²²And it shall come to pass, that ye shall divide it by lot for an inheritance unto you, and to the strangers that sojourn among you, which shall beget children among you: and they shall be unto you as born in the country among the children of Israel; they shall have inheritance with you among the tribes of Israel.[4]

In order to make His point clear as to the significance of the land, the Lord says in verse 13:

… I lifted up mine hand to give it unto your fathers: and this land shall fall unto you for inheritance.[5]

It is interesting to note two things in those words. First, God indicates he raised his hand in an oath that the land would be for the Israelites, a solumn commitment to the Jews. Second, this land shall fall unto you for inheritance, which indicates that the land would be obtained through war. When land is attained through a battle, it "falls" to the victorious.

Other Hebrew Scriptures stress the importance that God places on this land. In the first Book of the Bible, Genesis, the Lord appears to Abraham in Chapter 12 and says, *…Unto thy seed will I give this land.*

From this point, throughout the remainder of the Old Testament, this land becomes the focal point of God's prophetic revelations for Israel.

> *And the LORD appeared unto Abram, and said, Unto thy seed will I give this land: and there builded he an altar unto the LORD, who appeared unto him.*[6]

The commitment here states that the land will be handed down to the descendents of Abraham, the Jewish people today. It is an open-ended commitment, without a time limit.

Genesis 13:14:

> *And the LORD said unto Abram... Lift up now thine eyes, and look from the place where thou art northward, and southward, and eastward, and westward: For all the land which thou seest, to thee will I give it, and to thy seed for ever. ....Arise, walk through the land in the length of it and in the breadth of it; for I will give it unto thee.*[7]

God is laying out the area of land in question. It is large and encompasses all of present day Israel. This scripture also re-states the commitment that the land will be given to the descendants as a *permanent possession*.

Later, Isaac, the son of Abraham, hears the Lord re-state the commitment. Genesis 26:2:

> *Sojourn in this land, and I will be with thee, and will bless thee; for unto thee, and unto thy seed, I will give all these countries, and I will perform the oath which I sware unto Abraham thy father; And I will make thy seed to multiply as the stars of heaven...*[8]

In the following scripture, Isaac's son Jacob receives a dream from God relating to the land of Israel. The commitment given to Isaac is repeated to his son Jacob. As Jacob slept, he dreamed of a stairway that reached all the way to heaven. At the top of the stairway the Lord spoke to him. Genesis 28:13:

And, behold, the LORD stood above it, and said, I am the LORD God of Abraham thy father, and the God of Isaac: the land where-on thou liest, to thee will I give it, and to thy seed... And, behold, I am with thee, and will keep thee in all places whither thou goest, and will bring thee again into this land...[9]

Not long after this dream, God changed Jacob's name to Israel. And again restates His promise to Israel in Genesis 35:11:

And God said unto him, I am God Almighty: be fruitful and multiply; a nation and a company of nations shall be of thee, and kings shall come out of thy loins; And the land which I gave Abraham and Isaac, to thee I will give it, and to thy seed after thee will I give the land.[10]

It is clear from the Hebrew texts that God made a promise to the early fathers of the Jewish nation. He is giving the land to them and their descendants. The most basic understanding of the Hebrew Scriptures, relative to the Hebrews themselves, is recognition of the vital connection between a specific area of land and a specific people, the Jews, in special and covenant relationship with God.

In the modern era, the "Promised Land" came to Israel from war. Some of the land *fell* to Israel in the war for independence in 1948 and, then, more in the 1967 Six-Day War. In ancient times, Israel also acquired these lands in a series of battles. God promised to Moses two things; first that the Jewish captives would be set free from Egyptian bondage and, second, that He would bring them to a land of *milk and honey* that was to be their own. This second promise was fulfilled through war.

CONQUERING THE LAND OF CANAAN

Just about every nation in the world bases its claim to its land on some past military conquest, as any world history book can testify. In the case of the Jews, however, the claim to the land of Canaan is based on the belief that God promised them this land, which they then gained through military conquest. First, God fulfilled His promise to the Jews and freed them from Egypt. Then, He included lands that would be theirs. With such a promise from God, the children of Israel began traveling to the land of Canaan, described in God's promise as *milk and honey*.

En route, the leaders of Israel, Moses, Aaron, and Hur were confronted by a people called the Amalekites. They are led by their leader Amalek. There are two battles with this foe. The Jews lost the first one due to their disobedience to God. In the other battle, Amalek confronted the Israelites and launched a war to prevent them from proceeding further. By doing this, Amalek attempted to block God's promise to the Jews. Moses responds to the attack with one of his own. His goal is to create a passage through the desert, and his response is a frontal attack. Joshua, the leader of the Israeli forces, completely defeats the Amalekites. With this victory, Israel now has safe passage toward Canaan and the lands promised by God.[11] Now, with safe passage through the land of the Amalekites assured, Moses continues on and confronts the Southern Canaanites led by their leader, King Arad. Israel defeats the Canaanites and succeeds in taking the land promised by God. Moses also leads the Israelites into battle against Og, King of Basham. More of the land promised by God is taken as King Og and his sons are killed.[12]

Later, the Israeli leader Joshua battled the kings of Jerusalem, Hebron, Jarmuth, Lachish, and Eglon to secure more of the land promised to the Jews. He defeated them all. In yet another war for land, Joshua defeated the King of Libnah and also King Horam of Gezer. More land was taken from both peoples by Joshua for the Israelites.[13]

To take still more of the land that God promised the Israelites, Joshua led his armies against the King of Debir. This victory freed Israel from the threat of this king.

Then Joshua faced a brutal enemy in a gathering of many kings and peoples. These kings heard of the great Israeli victories and came together to defeat the Jewish people. But, the Israeli army is fulfilling a promise of God. There are nine kings and peoples-Madon, Shimron, Achshaph, North Mountains, South Mountains, the Canaanites, Amorites, Jabinites, and Hivites-and they represent a formidable army. Joshua's goal was to defend Israel and take more of the "Promised Land" in Northern Cannan. Here, as in other battles, Israel attacks suddenly and frontally, scoring a complete victory once again.[14, 15]

No nation of people was able to stand-up against the Jews when they fought for the "Promised Land" in fulfillment of God's promises. According to the ancient Hebrew texts, God made certain His promise was fulfilled. This method of land acquisition by a nation may displease the sensitivities of modern man, but only if he ignores his own history. Almost every modern country on the face of the Earth has been shaped by war, attaining land by conquest. And so it was in ancient times that Israel became a nation, out of the bondage of Egypt fulfilling all of what was told to Moses. After living in the "Promised Land" for centuries as the Jewish nations of Israel and Judah, the Jews were warned by the prophets that a great judgment was coming against them for their years of disobedience against God. They would be *scattered among the heathen* for many years to come. That message was truly frightening for an ancient people that believed the words of their prophets. But another, more pleasing, part to these dire warnings had to do with the eventual restoration of Israel in the distant future.

APPENDIX
B

The Year 1948 Predicted?

Many reject the notion that God will punish a nation of people. However, those that take this stance are often not familiar with the Bible. So the following narrative relating to the restoration of the nation of Israel to the "Promised Land" will be a difficult one for those that hold to this belief, even though it has an amazing result. As we saw in the previous chapter, Ezekiel prophesized that Israel would return to the "Promised Land" after being *scattered among the heathen*. This prophecy was made over 2500 years ago, and we know from recorded history that the Jewish people were *scattered among the heathen* only to reappear again as a nation in the year 1948. But Ezekiel went even further into detail concerning the rebirth of Israel. A good case can be made that he indicated the actual year of the rebirth, all the way from 2500 years ago!

This prophecy relating to the time when Israel would return to the land should help place in proper perspective the significance of what Ezekiel had to say. Also, it should highlight the importance of the "Promised Land," and why attempting to remove it from the Jews might result in a catastrophic event. This is important to establish before we begin looking at events that have transpired since 1991, catastrophes that began striking the United States that year, and then other nations as they too joined the effort to barter away the "Promised Land."

At this point it is necessary to have some basic understanding of Bible prophecy, even though that is not the point of this book. But to build the case for a connection to current United States foreign policy in the Middle East, and disasters that have been striking since 1991, it is first necessary to consider another prophecy concerning Israel. Long ago it was prophesized the Jews would lose their land and become spread among the nations, only to return again at some future time. But, to claim that the actual year of Israel's return was prophesized, that is another thing completely. It presses the imagination and it should, unless it can be established. Yet, based on writings from Ezekiel, it apparently can be established. Nevertheless, one must bear in mind that God does in fact punish the Jews for their disobedience throughout the ancient Hebrew writings.

Here are some important points to remember:

* God makes it clear in numerous Hebrew Scriptures that if Israel continues in its disobedience, He will "multiply their punishment by seven."

* The Jews had their own Hebrew calendar that consisted of a 360 day year.[1] Since we use the Julian calendar, we must convert the Jewish years to the correct number of 365.242 day years.

* When going from the year 1 B.C. to 1 A.D., there is no year 0 and we must add a year to the count.

Now let's look at the old Hebrew texts as they relate to the time when Israel was restored as a nation. We begin with the years of punishment that are determined against Israel for disobedience. This comes to us from other writings of Ezekiel and fits well with his "The Valley of Dry Bones" vision.

One of the key points to remember here is that Ezekiel writes much about the dispersion of the nation of Israel to the nations of the world, and its rebirth again as a nation. So it is not odd that he would be the one to tell us when this rebirth would take place....even the exact year!

Ezekiel is told to count the years that Israel has sinned against God. It is 390 for Israel, and 40 Judah. At that time, the Jewish nation was comprised of both states. Ezekiel chapter 4:

> *Lie thou also upon thy left side, and lay the iniquity of the house of Israel upon it: ... thou shalt bear their iniquity. For I have laid upon thee the years of their iniquity, according to the number of the days, three hundred and ninety days... Then, ...lie again on thy right side, and thou shalt bear the iniquity of the house of Judah forty days... each day for a year.[2]*

God is identifying to Ezekiel that attached to the nation of Israel, and its sister state Judah, are a total of 430 years of punishment. Then a few verses later in that same chapter:

> *And the LORD said, Even thus shall the children of Israel eat their defiled bread among the Gentiles, whither I will drive them.[3]*

In this text, it is made clear that the passage is referring to their dispersion among the Gentiles where God *will drive them.* Against the nation of Israel are 430 years of punishment to be experienced in Gentile lands. 390 years for the inequity of Israel and 40 years for that of Judah. Remember that total number of years of punishment: **430 years.**

We know from history that the Jews spend 70 years of captivity in Babylon, which ended in the year 537 B.C.* Therefore, those 70 years can be subtracted from the total years of punishment. This leaves a total punishment remaining now of **360 years.**

We must now look at a warning from God, that should Israel continue in its disobedience, He will multiply their punishment by seven times.

This is established by the following texts from one of the oldest writings found in the Jewish Torah, and again recorded in the Christian Old Testament. The Book of Leviticus:

> *And if ye will not yet for all this hearken unto me, then I will punish you seven times more for your sins.(26:18)*

> *And if ye walk contrary unto me, and will not hearken unto me; I will bring seven times more plagues upon you according to your sins.(26:21)*

> *And if ye will not for all this hearken unto me, but walk contrary unto me; Then I will walk contrary unto you also in fury; and I, even I, will chastise you seven times for your sins.(26:27-28)*

So now we have arrived at the following place as we march toward the year 1948. 360 years of punishment remain to be completed by the Jews after the first 70 years of punishment were completed in Babylon in the year 537 B.C.[5, 6, 7] We know from other texts in the Old Testament that the Jews continued to be disobedient in the eyes of God. So, it is safe to say they qualified themselves, based on these ancient Hebrew writings, for the remaining years of punishment to be multiplied by a factor of 7. 360 years of punishment multiplied by 7 tells us the nation of Israel would suffer punishment of exactly **2520 Jewish calendar years.**

There is now a simple conversion that needs to take place. The ancient Jewish calendar year had only 360 days in it. So to convert from Jewish years to our current Julian calendar, we multiply the 2520 Jewish years by their 360 days. That number is 907,200 days. Next, we simply divide 907,200 by the number of days in our calendar to determine the number of years based on the Julian calendar. When we divide 907,200 by 365.24 we get **2484 years.**

Now it gets even simpler. Starting with the year 537 B.C., the year that the initial 70 years of punishment was completed in captivity in Babylon, we add to it 2484 years and arrive at the year 1947. But, since there is no year 0 between 1 B.C and 1 A.D, we must add a year. We arrive at the year **1948**. It appears that old Ezekiel was indeed, the man who saw the future.

To sum it up:

430	Years of punishment shown to Ezekiel
-70	The years of punishment completed in Babylon
360	years of punishment remain against Israel
X 7	times is the number the punishment is multiplied for their continued disobedience.
2,520	Jewish Years
X360	Times days in the Jewish year
907,200	Total days of punishment according to the Hebrew writings
365.24	Number of Julian calendar days for division into modern years
2484	Julian calendar years of punishment

MINUS

537 B.C.	The year that the 70 years of captivity for Judah in Babylon was completed. This accounts for 70 of the
430	years of punishment and marks the beginning of the remaining 360 years.

EQUALS

1947	
+ 1	No year 0 in crossing from B.C. to A.D. add 1 year
1948	The year that the punishment ended and nation Israel was reborn

One of the most common questions people will ask is why God did not just say, "Israel will be reborn in the Julian calendar year 1948." Or, "the nation of Israel will begin to re-gather in the "promised land" in the immediate years following World War II," instead of making us piece it together. The answer is very simple. In studying the Hebrew Scriptures, it is apparent that God wants man to truly seek Him. Thus, if a man does not truly seek God with all of his heart by studying His words, he will never receive the reward of understanding. So those willing to pursue God will gain the benefit derived from that desire and see the accuracy of prophecy through study. Those not interested in pursuing this knowledge simply won't see it.

So here we have old Hebrew texts written over 2500 years ago that foretold a future for the nation of Israel that played out exactly as was indicated. The history that played out since Ezekiel recorded God's vision to him is historically indisputable. Historians will record that the nation of Israel saw its citizens, the Jews, cast throughout the world and dispersed *among the heathen*. But, then this great dispersion came to an end with the re-establishment of the nation of Israel in the exact year Ezekiel had foretold.

This brings us to the elephant in the room. If God was so interested in bringing this nation of people back into existence again after over 2000 years of wandering, even to the point of having His prophet provide the year of their return, then just how important does He view His promises as it relates to their possession of the "Promised Land?" One would reasonably think very important, which creates the basis of understanding in the chapters that describe the most severe disasters, and their uncanny timing connected with efforts to remove these "Promised Lands" from the possession of the Jews, and, therefore, reverse God's promise.

---

* The best historical consensus dates this event between 539-537 B.C. All of them place the return in a significant time frame of restoration. For the sake of this example, the year 537 B.C. is being used.

COINCIDENCES

OCTOBER 30, 1991

- Madrid Middle East Peace Conference opens its doors. It is a breakthrough that gets the warring parties talking, with the ultimate goal the removal of large portions of the "Promised Land"

- The worst of the "Perfect Storm" strikes the bewildered England coast, described by weather experts as a "once in a 100 year freak of nature."*

AUGUST 24, 1992

- Round six of the Madrid Peace effort begins in Washington D.C. with a new Israeli leader, Rabin at the helm. For the first time the "land for peace" effort has a friend on the Israeli side and significant progress is made.

- Hurricane Andrew, the 4th most powerful storm ever to make landfall in the U.S. strikes. It devastates South Florida becoming the most expensive natural disaster in the nation's history.*

APRIL 1993 UNTIL AUGUST 1993

- A historical peace agreement is negotiated over this time period, second only to the Camp David accord, it results in a removal of Israeli control over sections of the Promised Land"

- The "worst natural disaster in U.S. history" unfolds with several States inundated from continuous rains. Some say it was a 500 year flood, breaking records by the scores.*

JANUARY, 17 1994

- The day before President Clinton meets Syrian President Assad, they discuss the return of the Golan Heights from Israel. The following day Israeli Prime Minister Rabin warns the public to be prepared to return the Golan Heights.

- The highest ever recorded earthquake in an urban area strikes the U.S., causing the second most costly destruction caused by a natural disaster in U.S. history.*

JUNE 5, 2001

- The new Bush Administration begins with a "hands off" approach to the Middle East conflict. Then the White House suddenly announces it is sending CIA Director George Tenet in an effort to implement proposals that would restrict Israeli use of the "Promised Land"

- A tropical storm suddenly appears off the Texas coast, after "It went right from nothing to a tropical storm!" It strikes the Houston area resulting in what would be called the "Great flood of 2001"*

SEPTEMBER 10, 2001

- The week the Bush White House was ready for the "big rollout" of a major change in U.S. Middle East policy, becoming the first U.S. administration to support a Palestinian State on a large part of the "Promised Land."

- The next day, for the first time since Pearl Harbor, the U.S. is successfully attacked by a foreign enemy in a devastating assault.*

APRIL 30, 2003

- The "long awaited" effort by the Quartet was kicked-off on this day. This new effort included the United States, Russia, European Union, and the United Nations. The goal is centered on removing large portions of the "Promised Land" for the creation of a Palestinian State.

- The "worst weather in U.S. history" begins on this day, ultimately resulting in 562 tornados over a span of about 4 weeks, accompanied by 1,587 hail storms and 740 reports of additional wind damage.*

JUNE 2003 UNTIL AUGUST 2003

- Europe finally becomes an international player again and a major factor in the recent Quartet's effort to remove the "Promised Land" from Israel for the creation of a Palestinian State.

- The worst heat wave in over 250 years strikes Europe shortly after the "worst weather in U.S. history" ends. It devastates the continent with a terrible cost in lives.*

AUGUST 23, 2005

- The painful removal of Israeli citizens from large portions of the "Promised Land" is declared officially completed. Gaza is abandoned. About 5 months later Sharon is struck-down by a stroke. (NOTE: Old Jewish prophet Zaphaniah foretold a time would come when *"Gaza will be forsaken"*)

- Tropical depression number twelve is first noticed by the National Hurricane Center on this day. It is eventually named Katrina and soon becomes the most destructive natural disaster in U.S. history. Political advisors of President Bush, looking back at 2009, declare it was the beginning of the end of the Bush Presidency.*

WEEK OF JULY 23, 2007

- Former British Prime Minister Tony Blair begins his first trip to the Middle East as Quartet envoy, ultimately leading to the Annapolis Conference where the world begins a renewed effort to pressure the Jews to give up large portions of the "Promised Land" for a Palestinian state. (NOTE: Old Jewish prophet Zachariah foretold a group of four powers will divide the "Promised Land" resulting in terrifying events against the nations.)

- The world financial system suffers a critical breakdown, bringing it to the brink of a systemic meltdown. It all begins this week when the bank-to-bank loan premium begins an event statistically estimated should happen 1 day out of every 2,500,000.

* Coincidence was first identified by William Koenig in "Eye To Eye"

REFERENCES

PROLOGUE

1. Wikipedia Encyclopedia, "T.E. Lawrence," [accessed 08/08/09] http://en.wikipedia.org/wiki/T._E._Lawrence

2. First World War.com, [accessed 08/08/09] http://www.firstworldwar.com/

3. Wikipedia Encyclopedia, "Ottoman Empire," [accessed 08/09/09] http://en.wikipedia.org/wiki/Ottoman_Empire

4. Mideast Web, "Israel and Palestine: A Brief History," [accessed 08/09/09] http://www.mideastweb.org/briefhistory.htm

5. Wikipedia Encyclopedia, "Palestine," [accessed 08/09/09] http://en.wikipedia.org/wiki/Palestine

6. Ibid

7. Ibid

CHAPTER ONE

1. David Seltzer, *The Omen* {New York: New American Library, 1976}, pp 105

2. Bill Koenig, *Eye To Eye* {Aleandria, VA: About Him Publishing, 2008}

3. Wikipedia Encyclopedia, "Israel" [accessed 10/28/08] http://en.wikipedia.org/wiki/History_of_Israel

CHAPTER TWO

1. Wikipedia Encyclopedia, "Pythia" [accessed 8/21/09] http://en.wikipedia.org/wiki/Witch_of_Endor

2. Wikipedia Encyclopedia, "Witch of En Dor" [accessed 8/21/09] http://en.wikipedia.org/wiki/Pythia

3. *Holy Bible*, King James Version, Book of Ezekiel; Chapter 37

4. Ibid

5. Ibid

6. Ibid

7. Ibid

8. Ibid

9. Wikipedia Encyclopedia, *"1948 Arab-Israeli War"* [accessed 11/12/08] http://en.wikipedia.org/wiki/1948_Arab-Israeli_War

10. Ibid

11. Ibid

12. Ibid

13. Ibid

14. Michael Bard, "The 1948 War," Jewish Virtual Library, [accessed 11/13/08] http://www.jewishvirtuallibrary.org/jsource/History/1948_War.html

15. Ibid

16. Ibid

17. *Holy Bible*, King James Version, Book of Ezekiel; Chapter 36

18. *Holy Bible*, King James Version, Book of Ezekiel; Chapter 35

CHAPTER THREE

1. Gardiner, *The Admonitions of an Egyptian Sage*, (Georg Olms Verlag 1990) p. 7

2. James Long, *Riddle of the Exodus*, (Springdale AR: Lightcatcher Books, 2002) pp 93-103

3. *Holy Bible*, King James Version, Book of Exodus; Chapter 7

4. Gardiner, *The Admonitions of an Egyptian Sage*, (Georg Olms Verlag 1990)

5. *Holy Bible*, King James Version, Book of Exodus; Chapter 4

6. Gardiner, *The Admonitions of an Egyptian Sage*, (Georg Olms Verlag 1990)

7. *Holy Bible*, King James Version, Book of Exodus; Chapter 9

8. *Holy Bible*, King James Version, Book of Exodus; Chapter 10

9. Gardiner, *The Admonitions of an Egyptian Sage*, (Georg Olms Verlag 1990)

10. Ibid

11. Ibid

12. *Holy Bible*, King James Version, Book of Exodus; Chapter 10

13. Gardiner, *The Admonitions of an Egyptian Sage*, (Georg Olms Verlag 1990)

14. *Holy Bible*, King James Version, Book of Exodus; Chapter 12

15. Gardiner, The Admonitions of an Egyptian Sage, (Georg Olms Verlag 1990)

16. Ibid

17. Ibid

18. Ibid

19. *Holy Bible*, King James Version, Book of Exodus; Chapter 11

20. Gardiner, *The Admonitions of an Egyptian Sage*, (Georg Olms Verlag 1990)

21. Ibid

22. Ibid

23. Wikipedia Encyclopedia, "Khnum" [accessed 01/15/09] http:// en.wikipedia.org/wiki/Khnum

24. *Holy Bible*, King James Version, Book of Exodus; Chapter 13

25. Gardiner, *The Admonitions of an Egyptian Sage*, (Georg Olms Verlag 1990)

26. Wikipedia Encyclopedia, "El Arish" [accessed 8/24/09] http:// en.wikipedia.org/wiki/Arish

27. F.L. Griffith, *The Antiquities of Tell el Yahudiyeh and Miscellaneous Work in Lower Egypt during the Years 1887-1888* (London, , 1890)

28. Immanuel Velikovsky, *Ages in Chaos*, (New York, NY: Doubleday Books, 1956)

29. *Holy Bible*, King James Version, Book of Exodus; Chapter 10

30. F.L. Griffith, *The Antiquities of Tell el Yahudiyeh and Miscellaneous Work in Lower Egypt during the Years 1887-1888* (London, , 1890)

31. *Holy Bible*, King James Version, Book if Exodus; Chapter 14

32. Immanuel Velikovsky, *Ages in Chaos*, (New York, NY: Doubleday Books, 1956)

33. Ibid

CHAPTER FOUR

1. "Pre-Conference Diplomacy" Keesing's Record of World Events Volume 37, October, 1991 International, Page 38547

2. "Six Day War- 1967 Arab-Israeli War," [accessed 10/22/08] *www.sixdaywar.co.uk/*

3. James A. Baker, III, *The Politics of Diplomacy, Revolution, War & Peace, 1989-1992* (New York: G.P. Putnam's and Sons), 1995;

4. *"The 'Perfect' storm: Bob Case," USA Today*, [accessed 10/10/08] www.usatoday.com/community/chat/0706case.htm

5. A&E Television, This Day in History 1991: [accessed 12/22/08] "Perfect Storm hits North Atlantic" October 30, 1991

6. Sebastian Junger, *The Perfect Storm*, {New York, NY: WW Norton & Company, 1997}

7. History Central, "America's Wars—Operation Desert Storm," [accessed 10/28/08] http://www.historycentral.com/desert_storm/

8. Ursula Grosser Dixon, "Ode To Joy and Freedom-The Fall of the Berlin Wall," [accessed 11/03/08] http://nevermore.tripod.com/wall.html

9. United Nations---Security Council, "Question of Palestine," [accessed 11/21/08] http://www.un.org/depts/dpa/qpalnew/security_council.htm

10. CNN.com *"The actual Perfect Storm: A perfectly dreadful combination of nature's forces"* [accessed 10/30/08] http://archives.cnn.com/2000/NATURE/06/30/perfect.storm/ [accessed January 3, 2009]

11. Wikipedia Encyclopedia, "UN Security Council Resolutions 242 & 338" [accessed 01/02/09] *en.wikipedia.org/wiki/United_Nations_Security_Council_Resolution_242 - 97k –*

12. Stein, Kenneth W. (1991). *Madrid Middle East Peace Conference, October 30-November 2, 1991,* Emory University Institute for the Study of Modern Israel

13. McGuinness, Tim, "Deadly Storms" Unnamed Hurricane "The Perfect Storm" *1991* [accessed 11/07/08] www.DeadlyStorms.com

14. American Experiences, "Timeline- George H.W. Bush," [accessed 12/04/08] http://www.pbs.org/wgbh/amex/bush41/timeline/

15. The Perfect Storm Foundation, "History of the Perfect Storm" [accessed 02/10/09] http://www.perfectstorm.org/storms.cfm

16. Bill Koenig, Eye To Eye {Alexandria, VA: About Him Publishing, 2008}

Chapter Five

1. Dan Kurzman *Soldier of Peace, The Life of Yitzhak Rabin* (New York: Harper Collins, 1998)

2. Wikipedia Encyclopedia, "Hurricane Andrew'" [accessed 02/02/2009] http://en.wikipedia.org/wiki/Hurricane_Andrew

3. Ibid

4. **"Hurricane Andrew-August 24, 1992,"** *The Miami Herald,* [accessed April 26, 2009] www.geocities.com/hurricanene/hurricaneandrew.htm

5. *Seattle Times,* "Land For Peace—Rabin Puts Golan Heights On The Table With Syria," [accessed 11/9/2008] http://seattletimes.nwsource.com/cgi-bin/PrintStory.pl?slug=1513116&date=19920915

6. Bronner, Ethan, "Rabin offers Syria land for peace, Would yield part of Golan Heights" *The Boston Globe,* September 11, 1992 "Land for Peace" http://www.nationmaster.com/encyclopedia/land-for-peace [accessed November 10, 2008]

7. CNN "Anti-Rabin sentiment had turned ugly" Article date: November 5, 1995 http://www.cnn.com/world/9511/rabin/why_now/index.html [accessed 10/05/08]

8. **"Thousands gather to mark 13 years since Rabin shot,"** *USA Today*, 11/8/2008 [accessed 11/9/2008] http://www.usatoday.com/news/world/2008-11-08-israel-rabin-rally_N.htm

9. Wikipedia Encyclopedia, "Hurricane Andrew'" [accessed 02/02/2009] http://en.wikipedia.org/wiki/Hurricane_Andrew

10. Ibid

11. CBS, "Brian Norcross Recalls The Storm—Hurricane Andrew 15 Years Later: Lessons Learned," 8/23/2007 [accessed 11/14/2008] http://cbs4.com/history/hurricane.andrew.bryan.2.405166.html

12. Janet McDonnell, "Hurricane Andrew Historical Report," Office of History-US Army Corps of Engineers, January 1993

13. **"Washington bilateral negotiations," Keesing's Record of World Events, International Volume 38, [August, 1992] Page 39070**

14. World & Nation, International, *The Buffalo News* "Rabin's assassin says peace deal led to act," November 01, 2008 http://www.buffalonews.com/nationalworld/international/story/480615.html

15. Israeli Ministry of Foreign Affairs, "Israel's Peace-Making Policies on the eve of the Renewal of Bilateral Talks", Jerusalem, August 18, 1992 http://www.mfa.gov.il/MFA/Archive/Peace%20Process/1992/ISRAEL-S%20PEACE-MAKING%20POLICIES%20ON%20THE%20EVE%20OF%20THE%20R

16. Time in partnership with CNN "Some Land for Peace" September 21, 1992 [accessed 01/29/09] http://www.time.com/time/magazine/article/0,9171,976536,00.html

17. Ibid

18. Wikipedia Encyclopedia, "Hurricane Andrew" [accessed 02/02/2009] http://en.wikipedia.org/wiki/Hurricane_Andrew

19. NOAA, National Weather Service, "Hurricane History," [accessed 8/24/09] http://www.nhc.noaa.gov/HAW2/english/history.shtml

20. Special Report, *St Petersburg Times,* "Hurricane Andrew-After the Storm" August 24, 2002 http://www.sptimes.com/2002/webspecials02/andrew/

21. Robert Pear, "Hurricane Andrew; Breakdown Seen in U.S. Storm Aid," *The New York Times*, August 29, 1992 [accessed 4/26/2009] www.nytimes.com/1992/08/29/us/hurricane-andrew-breakdown-seen-in-us-storm-aid.html?

22. Bill Koenig, Eye To Eye {Alexandria, VA: About Him Publishing, 2008}

CHAPTER SIX

1. Wikipedia Encyclopedia, "Camp David Accords" [accessed 8/24/09] http://en.wikipedia.org/wiki/Camp_David_Accords

2. U.S. Department of State 93/04/21 News Conference on Middle East Peace Talks To Resume, Washington D.C.

3. U.S. Department of State 93/03/10 News Conference on Resumption of Middle East Peace Negotiations, Washington D.C.

4. Nation Master Encyclopedia, s.v. "1993 Oslo Peace Accords between Palestinians and Israel" http://www.nationmaster.com/encyclopedia/1993-Oslo-Peace-Accords-between-Palestinians-and-Israel [accessed 12/01/08]

5. Adam Pitluk, "Revising the Great Flood of 1993 and James Scott," Huffington Post, 12 June 2007, http://www.huffingtonpost.com/adam-pitluk/revisiting-the-great-floo_b_51842.html?view=print [accessed 04/28/09]

6. NOAA, National Weather Service, Office of Hydrology "The Great Flood of 1993," Lee W. Larson, Silver Spring, Maryland http://www.engr.colostate.edu/~jsalas/us-italy/abstract/11.htm [accessed 11/22/08]

7. "Statistics, Stories, and Chronology from the Great Mississippi River Flood of 1993," "1993 Mississippi Flood CHRONOLOGY" http://www.greatriver.com/FLOOD.htm [accessed 12/17/08]

8. Mideast & N. Africa Encyclopedia, s.v., Oslo Accord (1993) http://www.answers.com/topic/oslo-accords [accessed 11/22/08]

9. The Online News Hour, "Israeli-Palestinian Conflict," Oslo Accord, September 13,1993 http://www.pbs.org/newshour/indepth_coverage/middle_east/conflict/peaceefforts3.html [accessed 12/12/08]

10. Joel Singer, "Middle Ease Briefing," *Middle East Quarterly*, March 19, 1997

11. *History Channel*, This Day In History, "Israel-Palestine peace accord signed" September 13, 1993 http://www.history.com/this-day-in-history.do?action=Article&id=7019 , [accessed 12/10/08]

12. NOAA/National Weather Service Central Region, "Quiet Beginning Heralded Nation's Worst Flood In 1993," Patrick Slattery, http://www.noaanews.noaa.gov/stories/s1125.htm [accessed 04/28/09]

13. Robert Britt, "History Repeats: The Great Flood of 1993" *Live Science* Managing Editor 22 June 2008 http://www.livescience.com/environment/080622-great-flood-1993.html [accessed 11/01/08]

14. NOAA/National Weather Service, Office of Hydrology, "The Great Flood of 1993" LEE W. LARSON, Silver Spring, Maryland http://www.nwrfc.noaa.gov/floods/papers/oh_2/great.htm [accessed 01/22/09]

15. U.S. Embassy, Israel, "Clinton Speech" [accessed 8/24/09] http://usembassy-israel.org.il/publish/peace/archives/2001/january/me0108b.html

16. Nation Master Encyclopedia, s.v. "1993 Oslo Peace Accords between Palestinians and Israel" http://www.nationmaster.com/encyclopedia/1993-Oslo-Peace-Accords-between-Palestinians-and-Israel [accessed 12/01/08]

17. The Online News Hour, "Israeli-Palestinian Conflict," Oslo Accord, September 13,1993 http://www.pbs.org/newshour/indepth_coverage/middle_east/conflict/peaceefforts3.html [accessed 12/12/08]

18. *History Channel*, This Day In History, "Israel-Palestine peace accord signed" September 13, 1993 http://www.history.com/this-day-in-history.do?action=Article&id=7019 , [accessed 12/10/08]

19. Adam Pitluk, "Revising the Great Flood of 1993 and James Scott," Huffington Post, 12 June 2007, http://www.huffingtonpost.com/adam-pitluk/revisiting-the-great-floo_b_51842.html?view=print [accessed 04/28/09]

20. Ibid

21. NOAA/National Weather Service, Office of Hydrology, "The Great Flood of 1993" LEE W. LARSON, Silver Spring, Maryland http://www.nwrfc.noaa.gov/floods/papers/oh_2/great.htm [accessed 01/22/09]

22. NOAA/National Weather Service, Office of Hydrology, Quiet Beginning **Heralded** the Nations Worst Flood, [accessed 3/19/09] http://www.noaanews.noaa.gov/stories/s1125.htm

23. Adam Pitluk, "Revising the Great Flood of 1993 and James Scott," Huffington Post, 12 June 2007, http://www.huffingtonpost.com/adam-pitluk/revisiting-the-great-floo_b_51842.html?view=print [accessed 04/28/09]

24. Nobelprize.org, "The Nobel Peace Prize 1994" [accessed 8/24/09] http://nobelprize.org/nobel_prizes/peace/laureates/1994/press.html

25. Michael Lewis, "Israel's American Detractors - Back Again, A Very Bad Agreement, but the Only Agreement Possible," *Middle East Quarterly* December 1997

26. Bill Koenig, Eye To Eye {Alexandria, VA: About Him Publishing, 2008}

CHAPTER SEVEN

1. Wikipedia Encyclopedia, "Six-Day War" [accessed 8/24/09] http://en.wikipedia.org/wiki/Six-Day_War

2. Wikipedia Encyclopedia, "Golan Heights" [accessed 8/24/09] http://en.wikipedia.org/wiki/Golan_Heights

3. Bible Places "Golan Heights" (Biblical Beshan) http://www.bibleplaces.com/golanheights.htm

4. Arab-Israeli War of 1973—MSN Encarta http://encarta.msn.com/encyclopedia_761564886/arab-israeli_war_of_1973.html

5. Ibid

6. Ronald Reagan, House of Commons, London, England, March 8, 1983 National Center Archives http://www.nationalcenter.org/ReaganEvilEmpire1983.html

7. The Cold War Museum, "Fall of the Soviet Union," [accessed 02/02/09] http://www.coldwar.org/articles/90s/fall_of_the_soviet_union.asp

8. Arab-Israeli War of 1973—MSN Encarta http://encarta.msn.com/encyclopedia_761564886/arab-israeli_war_of_1973.html

9. Keesing's Record of World Events Volume 40, January, 1994 International, Page 39837

10. *New York Times* "Rabin says Peace with Syria may require painful price By Clyde Haberman 01/19/1994 Issue

11. Wikipedia Encyclopedia, "1994 Northridge Earthquake" http://en.wikipedia.org/wiki/Northridge_earthquake

12. Earthquake Engineering Research Center Northridge Earthquake http://nisee.berkeley.edu/northridge

13. EQE International "Northridge Earthquake" http://www.lafire.com/famous_fires/940117_NorthridgeEarthquake/quake/01_EQE_exsummary.htm

14. *Holy Bible*, King James Version, Book if Ezekiel; Chapter 37

15. Bill Koenig, Eye To Eye {Alexandria, VA: About Him Publishing, 2008}

CHAPTER EIGHT

1. Zak Mazur, UWM Post, "Hamas not to be Trusted" www.uwmpost.com/article/c58b6a040942a99001094d2534b80034

2. Middle East Facts, "Arafat in Stockholm," [accessed 2/2/2009] http://www.middleeastfacts.com/Articles/arafat-in-stockholm.php

3. Zionist Organization of America, "New Poll: Palestinians Support Suicide Bombings By 55% To 37%," [accessed 2/7/2009] www.zoa.org/sitedocuments/pressrelease_view.asp?pressreleaseID=1577

4. Daniel Pipes, Israeli Insider, "Polls, Palestinians and the path to peace," [accessed [2/6/2009] http://web.israelinsider.com/bin/en.jsp?enPage=ViewsPage&enDisplay=view&enDispWhat=object&enDispWho=Article^l1992&enZone=Views&enVersion=0&

5. *Haaretz News*, "Poll: Most Palestinians think Hamas should not recognize Israel," [accessed 2/2/2009] http://www.haaretz.com/hasen/spages/764368.html

6. Sharm El-Sheikh Fact Finding Committee, "Mitchell Report," Suleyman Demirel, Thorbjoern Jagland , Warren B. Rudman , Javier Solana, George J Mitchell, http://www.globalpolicy.org/security/issues/israel-palestine/document/mitchell043001.pdf, [accessed 02/02/09]

7. Daniel Pipes, "Mitchell Report Missed it", *Washington Times*, 05/30/2001, http://www.danielpipes.org/article/380, [accessed 02/02/09]

8. Alan Sipress, "Tenet Returns to Middle East To Rejoin Talks on Security," *Washington Post*, http://www.washingtonpost.com/ac2/wp-dyn/A25386-2001Jun5?language=printer

9. Mouin Rabbani, "The Mitchell Report: Oslo's Last Gasp," Middle East Desk [accessed 3/1/2009] http://www.merip.org/mero/mero060101.html

10. Phil Reeves, "Revealed: US-led commission on Middle East troubles urges end to building in occupied territories," *The Independent*, 05/05/2001, http://www.independent.co.uk/news/world/middle-east/halt-all-settlements-israel-is-told-753962.html, [accessed 02/02/09]

11. Israel Ministry of Foreign Affairs, Israel's Comments on the Mitchell Committee Report, May 15, 2001, [accessed 02/02/09] http://www.mfa.gov.il/MFA/MFAArchive/2000_2009/2001/5/Israel-s%20Comments%20on%20the%20Mitchell%20Committee%20Report, [accessed 02/02/09]

12. Ami Isseroff, "The Peace Process is Dead, Long Live the Peace Process," Middle East Web, January 17, 2003 [accessed 12/01/08] http://www.mideastweb.org/oslofailed.htm

13. Eric Berger & Tony Freemantle, "Tropical Storm Allison threatens Texas and Louisiana coasts," *Houston Chronicle*, June 9, 2001 [accessed 2/26/2009] www.chron.com/disp/story.mpl/storm2001/930916.html

14. Eric Berger & Tony Freemantle, "Tropical Surprise Floods area," *Houston Chronicle*, June 6, 2001 [accessed 2/26/2009] www.chron.com/disp/story.mpl/storm2001/931972.html

15. Eric Berger & Tony Freemantle, "Tropical Storm Allison threatens Texas and Louisiana coasts," *Houston Chronicle*, June 9, 2001 [accessed 2/26/2009] www.chron.com/disp/story.mpl/storm2001/930916.html

16. Eric Berger, "Inside Allison's Bag of Tricks," *Houston Chronicle*, June 7, 2001 [accessed 2/26/2009] www.chron.com/disp/story.mpl/storm2001/934398.html

17. Eric Berger & Tony Freemantle, "Tropical Storm Allison threatens Texas and Louisiana coasts," *Houston Chronicle*, June 9, 2001 [accessed 2/26/2009] www.chron.com/disp/story.mpl/storm2001/930916.html

18. Eric Berger & Tony Freemantle, "Tropical surprise floods area," *Houston Chronicle*, June 6, 2001 [accessed 2/26/2009] www.chron.com/disp/story.mpl/storm2001/931972.html

19. Dan Feldstein, "Tropical earns spot in storm history," *Houston Chronicle*, June 9, 2001 [accessed 2/26/2009] www.chron.com/disp/story.mpl/storm2001/936857.html

20. Associated Press, "Allison's wrath prompts name retirement", *Houston Chronicle*, July 6, 2002, http://www.chron.com/disp/story.mpl/stprm2001/1485169.html [accessed 02/02/09]

21. "Allison: A Historical Perspective", *Houston Chronicle,*" http://www.chron.com/content/news/photos/01/06/24/allisoncompared/popup2.htm, [accessed 12/01/08]

22. Bill Koenig, Eye To Eye {Alexandria, VA: About Him Publishing, 2008}

CHAPTER NINE

1. "Arab Oil Embargo," Palestine Facts, [accessed 3/13/2009] http://www.palestinefacts.org/pf_1967to1991_oilembargo_result.php

2. Wikipedia Encyclopedia, "1973 Oil Crisis," [accessed 3/21/2009] http://en.wikipedia.org/wiki/Arab_Oil_Embargo

3. CRS Report to Congress, "The Islamic Traditions of Wahhabism and Salafiyya" [accessed 8/24/09] http://www.fas.org/sgp/crs/misc/RS21695.pdf

4. Michael Isikoff & Daniel Klaidman, "The Hijackers We Let Escape," *Newsweek* [06/10/02] http://www.newsweek.com/id/64762/output/print [accessed 05/03/09]

5. Jeffrey Smith, "A History of Missed Connections," *Washington Post*, July 25, 2003, http://www.washingtonpost.com/ac2/wp-dyn/A43165-2003Jul24?language=printer [accessed 05/03/09]

6. Bob Woodward, *State of Denial,* (New York: Simon & Schuster, 2006) pp. 76-78

7. Robert Kaiser & David Ottoway, "Marriage of Convenience," Series of three articles, *Washington Post*, 02/10/2002

8. "Bush Sr. Assures Crown Prince Abdullah that Bush Jr's 'Heart Is in Right Place'", *History Commons*, July 2001, http://www.historycommons.org/context.jsp?item=western_support_for_islamic_militancy_2847 [accessed 12/12/08]

9. Roger Hardy, "Saudi anger at US silence," *History Commons*, [November 9, 2001] www.HistoryCommons.org, [accessed 12/12/08]

10. "August 27, 2001: Saudis Threaten to End Their Alliance with US", *History Commons*, www.HistoryCommons.org, [accessed 12/12/08]

11. "Palestine", *Keesing's Record of World Events"-September 2001 International*, Volume 47, pp 44371

12. Michael Isikoff & Daniel Klaidman, "The Hijackers We Let Escape," *Newsweek* [06/10/02] http://www.newsweek.com/id/64762/output/print [accessed 05/03/09]

13. Jeffrey Smith, "A History of Missed Connections," *Washington Post*, July 25, 2003, http://www.washingtonpost.com/ac2/wp-dyn/A43165-2003Jul24?language=printer [accessed 05/03/09]

14. "Saudis Threaten To end their Alliance with US," & "Crown Prince Abdullah Warns Bush Against Pro-Israel Stance in Letter", *History Commons*, August 2001, http://www.historycommons.org/context.jsp?item=western_support_for_islamic_militancy_2847 [accessed 12/12/08]

15. Robert Kaiser & David Ottoway, "Marriage of Convenience," Series of three articles, *Washington Post*, 02/10/2002

16. Bob Woodward, *State of Denial,* (New York: Simon & Schuster, 2006)

17. "Saudis Threaten To end their Alliance with US," & "Crown Prince Abdullah Warns Bush Against Pro-Israel Stance in Letter", *History Commons*, August 2001, http://www.historycommons.org/context.jsp?item=western_support_for_islamic_militancy_2847 [accessed 12/12/08]

18. Bob Woodward, *State of Denial,* (New York: Simon & Schuster, 2006)

19. Ibid

20. Robert Kaiser & David Ottoway, "Marriage of Convenience," Series of three articles, *Washington Post*, 02/10/2002

21. Ibid

22. Bob Woodward, *State of Denial,* (New York: Simon & Schuster, 2006)

23. Michael Isikoff & Daniel Klaidman, "The Hijackers We Let Escape," *Newsweek* [06/10/02] http://www.newsweek.com/id/64762/output/print [accessed 05/03/09]

24. Jeffrey Smith, "A History of Missed Connections," *Washington Post*, July 25, 2003, http://www.washingtonpost.com/ac2/wp-dyn/A43165-2003Jul24?language=printer [accessed 05/03/09]

25. Bob Woodward, *State of Denial,* (New York: Simon & Schuster, 2006)

26. August 29-September 6, 2001: Bush Tries to Repair Relations with Saudis, But Policy Change Halted by 9/11 Attacks," History Commons, www. HistoryCommons.org, [accessed 12/12/08]

27. Jeffrey Smith, "A History of Missed Connections," *Washington Post*, July 25, 2003, http://www.washingtonpost.com/ac2/wp-dyn/A43165-2003Jul24?language=printer [accessed 05/03/09]

28. Bob Woodward, *State of Denial,* (New York: Simon & Schuster, 2006) pp. 76-78

29. Ibid

30. Jeffrey Smith, "A History of Missed Connections," *Washington Post*, July 25, 2003, http://www.washingtonpost.com/ac2/wp-dyn/A43165-2003Jul24?language=printer [accessed 05/03/09]

31. Wikipedia Encyclopedia, "September 11, 2001 Attacks," http:// en.wikipedia.org/wiki/September_11,_2001_attacks, [accessed 12/12/08]

32. William Koenig, *Eye To Eye*, (Alexandria, VA: About Him, 2008) pp. 100-101

33. Bill Koenig, Eye To Eye {Alexandria, VA: About Him Publishing, 2008}

CHAPTER TEN

1. Daniel Mandel, "Four-Part Disharmony: The Quartet Maps Peace," *Middle East Quarterly*, Summer 2003

2. Ibid

3. Ibid

4. "President Discusses Roadmap for Peace in the Middle East," Remarks By The President on the Middle East, The Rose Garden, www.whitehouse.gov/ news/releases/2003/03/2003014-4.html

5. Wikipedia Encyclopedia, "Road map for peace," [accessed 11/23/2008] http://en.wikipedia.org/wiki/Road_map_for_peace

6. Wikipedia Encyclopedia, "Ariel Sharon," [accessed 11/29/2008] http:// en.wikipedia.org/wiki/Ariel_Sharon

7. Wikipedia Encyclopedia, "Mahmoud Abbas," [accessed 11/29/2008] http://en.wikipedia.org/wiki/Mahmoud_Abbas

8. Frontline World, "The Rise of Hamas" [accessed 8/24/09] http://www.pbs. org/frontlineworld/stories/palestine503/history.html

9. *Holy Bible*, King James Version, Book of Ezekiel; Chapter 35

10. "President Discusses Roadmap for Peace in the Middle East," Remarks By The President on the Middle East, The Rose Garden, www.whitehouse.gov/ news/releases/2003/03/2003014-4.html

11. Wikipedia Encyclopedia, "Israel–United States relations," [accessed 12/01/2008] http://en.wikipedia.org/wiki/Israel-United_States_relations

12. "Joint Statement by the Quartet – The Road Map," 4/30/2003, www.europa-eu-un.org/atricles/en/article_2283_en.htm

13. US State Department, "A Performance-Based Roadmap to a Permanent Two-State Solution to the Israeli-Palestinian Conflict," Washington D.C., April 30, 2003 [accessed 11/21/2008] http://www.state.gov/r/pa/prs/ps/2003/20062.htm

14. Wikipedia Encyclopedia, Redirected to *Science Daily*, "May 2003 tornado outbreak sequence," [accessed 12/03/2008 http://www.sciencedaily.com/articles/m/may_2003_tornado_outbreak_sequence.htm

15. Ann Patton, Surviving the Storm: Sheltering in the May 2003 Tornados in Moore, Oklahoma," University of Colorado, [accessed 12/12/2008] http://www.colorado.edu/hazards/research/qr/qr163/qr163.pdf

16. NOOA National Weather Service, "Record Number of Tornados, NOAA Reports" [accessed 12/02/2008] http://www.noaanews.noaa.gov/stories/s1144.htm

17. *Science Daily*, "May 2003 Tornado Outbreak Sequence," [accessed 1/12/2009] http://www.sciencedaily.com/articles/m/may_2003_tornado_outbreak_sequence.htm

18. Bill Koenig, Eye To Eye {Alexandria, VA: About Him Publishing, 2008}

CHAPTER ELEVEN

1. Wikipedia Encyclopedia, "Treaties of Rome," [accessed 01/14/2009] http://en.wikipedia.org/wiki/Treaty_of_Rome

2. BBC History, "World War One," [accessed 01/22/2009] http://www.bbc.co.uk/history/worldwars/wwone/

3. BBC History, "World War Two," [accessed 01/22/2009] www.bbc.co.uk/history/worldwars/wwtwo

4. Ibid

5. BBC History, "World War One," [accessed 01/22/2009] http://www.bbc.co.uk/history/worldwars/wwone/

6. GlobalSecurity.org, "Cold War" [accessed 8/24/09] http://www.globalsecurity.org/military/ops/cold_war.htm

7. Wikipedia Encyclopedia, "Treaties of Rome," [accessed 01/14/2009] http://en.wikipedia.org/wiki/Treaty_of_Rome

8. Historiasiglo20.org, "The History of the European Union," [accessed 01/15/2009] http://www.historiasiglo20.org/europe/traroma.htm

9. BBC News, "EU Pushes for Mid-East roadmap, [accessed 01/22/2009] http://news.bbc.co.uk/2/hi/middle_east/3032891.stm

10. Javier Solana Statement, "Javier Solana, EU High Representative for the Common Foreign and Security Policy, welcomes the approval of the Palestinian Authority's Prime Minister and his cabinet," Brussels April 29, 2003 [accessed 03/06/2009] http://www.consilium.europa.eu/ueDocs/cms_Data/docs/pressdata/EN/declarations/75574.pdf

11. Bush Statement---"President Discusses Roadmap for Peace in the Middle East" Rose Garden White House April 30, 2003 http://www.whitehouse.gov/news/releases/2003/03/20030314-4.html

12. "EU pushes for Mid-East roadmap," BBC News, 05/16/2003 http://news.bbc.co.uk/go/pr/fr/-/2/hi/middle_east/3032891.stm [accessed 2/20/2009]

13. "Joint Statement by the Quartet-The Road Map," European Union @ United Nations, April 30, 2003, [accessed 02/23/2009] http://www.europa-eu-un.org/articles/en/article_2283_en.htm

14. *Holy Bible*, King James Version, Book of Ezekiel; Chapter 37

15. Kessing's Record of World Events, "Palestine," Volume 49, May, 2003 International Page 45439 & 45378

16. "Climate and weather in France," About France, [accessed 4/14/2009] http://about-france.com/climate-weather.htm

17. William Manchester, "Alone-The Last Lion," (London, England: Little, Brown and Company, 1988) pp 499

18. United Nations Environment Programme-Environmental Alert Bulletin, "Impacts of summer 2003 heat wave in Europe," [accessed 02/10/2009 http://www.grid.unep.ch/product/publication/download/ew_heat_wave.en.pdf

19. Wikipedia Encyclopedia, "2003 European heat wave," [accessed 02/11/2009] http://en.wikipedia.org/wiki/2003_European_heat_wave

20. Ibid

21. Ibid

22. Ibid

23. Earth Policy Institute, "Record Heat Wave in Europe Takes 35,000 Lives: Far Greater Losses May Lie Ahead," [accessed 06/04/2009] http://www.earth-policy.org/Updates/Update29.htm

24. Earth Policy Institute, "Setting The Record Straight: More than 52,000 Europeans Died from Heat in Summer 2003," 07/28/2006 http://www.earth-policy.org/Updates/2006/Update56.htm [accessed 02/14/2009]

25. Ibid

26. United Nations Environment Programme-Environmental Alert Bulletin, "Impacts of summer 2003 heat wave in Europe," [accessed 02/10/2009 http://www.grid.unep.ch/product/publication/download/ew_heat_wave.en.pdf

27. Wikipedia Encyclopedia, "2003 European heat wave," [accessed 02/11/2009] http://en.wikipedia.org/wiki/2003_European_heat_wave

28. Jason R. Webster, "The European Heat Wave & Drought Event of 2003," Creighton University-Department of Atmospheric Sciences-20th Conference on Climate Variability and Change," [accessed 02/09/2009] http://www.jasonrwebster.com/resources/European+Heat+Wave+$26+Drought+Event+of+2003+-1.pdf

29. Voice of America, "Record Breaking Heat Wave Scorches Europe," 08/05/2003 [accessed 02/05/2009] http://www.voanews.com/english/archive/2003-08/a-2003-08-05-27-record.cfm

30. Earth Policy Institute, "Setting The Record Straight: More than 52,000 Europeans Died from Heat in Summer 2003," 07/28/2006 http://www.earth-policy.org/Updates/2006/Update56.htm [accessed 02/14/2009]

31. Bill Koenig, Eye To Eye {Alexandria, VA: About Him Publishing, 2008}

CHAPTER TWELVE

1. CNN, "Violence hits Gaza pullout—Historic Gaza withdrawal began on the stroke of midnight," 8/15/08, http://www.cnn.com/2005/WORLD/meast/08/14/gaza.pullout/index.html

2. Ibid

3. Ibid

4. Ibid

5. Voice of America, "Israel Begins Forced Evacuation of Gaza Settlers," 8/17/08

6. *Jerusalem Post*, Gaza Evacuations, August 17, 2005 (noted on Slate: http://www.slate.com/id/2124599)

7. "Gaza settlement evacuation complete, Israel says," *The Sydney Morning Herald*, 08/23/2005, [accessed 03/03/2009] http://www.smh.com.au/news/world/gaza-settlement-evacuation-complete-israel-says/2005/08/23/1124562813714.html

8. "Israel Completes Evacuation of Gaza and West Bank Settlers" *New York Times* http://www.nytimes.com/2005/08/23/international/middleeast/23cnd-settlers.html?ei=5090&en=5b6659e88b9d3763&ex=1282449600&partner=rssuscrland&emc=rss&pagewanted=print

9. Slate, "Leaving Gaze, The Middle East Press looks at Israel's withdrawal" [3/28/09] http://www.slate.com/id/2124599

10. *Holy Bible*, King James Version, Book of Zephaniah, Chapter 2

11. Finis Dake, *Dake's Annotated Reference Bible*, (Lawrenceville, GA: Dake Publishing 2004)

12. *Haaretz News Service*, "30 Gaza rockets strike Negev, one person lightly wounded," 01/10/2009 [accessed 03/02/2009] http://www.haaretz.com/hasen/spages/1054188.html

13. Ibid

14. Seymour Gitin, Trude Dothan, Joseph Naveh, Special Report: Ekron Identity Confirmed," *Archaeology*, Archaeological Institute of America, [accessed 3/2/2009] http://www.archaeology.org/9801/abstracts/ekron.html

15. *Haaretz News Service*, "30 Gaza rockets strike Negev, one person lightly wounded," 01/10/2009 [accessed 03/02/2009] http://www.haaretz.com/hasen/spages/1054188.html

16. Wikipedia Encyclopedia, "Hurricane Katrina," [accessed 02/03/2009] http://en.wikipedia.org/wiki/Meteorological_history_of_Hurricane_Katrina

17. CNN.com, "New Orleans braces for monster hurricane," [8/29/05, [accessed 3/13/09] http://www.cnn.com/2005/WEATHER/08/28/hurricane.katrina/

18. Ibid

19. NOAA, "Hurricane History," [accessed 02/10/2009] http://www.nhc.noaa.gov/HAW2/english/history.shtml

20. Associated Press-MSNBC, "Ex-Bush aides: He didn't recover from Katrina," 12/30/2008 MSNBC.com, The Associated Press 12/30/08 [accessed 02/08/2009] http://www.msnbc.msn.com/id/28433687/

21. Ibid

22. Wikipedia Encyclopedia, "Ariel Sharon" [accessed 02/21/09] http://en.wikipedia.org/wiki/Ariel_Sharon

23. Bill Koenig, Eye To Eye {Alexandria, VA: About Him Publishing, 2008}

CHAPTER THIRTEEN

1. Wikipedia Encyclopedia, "Qassam Rocket," Israel, [accessed 04/22/09] http://en.wikipedia.org/wiki/File:Qasam_graph2002-2007.svg

2. Ibid

3. Wikipedia Encyclopedia, "Battle of Gaza 2007," [accessed 4/22/09] http://en.wikipedia.org/wiki/Battle_of_Gaza_(2007)

4. Jewish Virtual Library, "Peace Treaty Between Israel and Egypt," 03/29/1979 [accessed 03/12/2009] http://www.jewishvirtuallibrary.org/jsource/Peace/egypt-israel_treaty.html

5. Ibid

6. Wikipedia Encyclopedia, "Rafah Border Crossing," [accessed 04/29/09] http://en.wikipedia.org/wiki/Rafah_Border_Crossing

7. Wikipedia Encyclopedia, "Qassam Rocket," Israel, [accessed 04/22/09] http://en.wikipedia.org/wiki/File:Qasam_graph2002-2007.svg

8. Carolynne Wheeler & Megan Levy, *Daily Telegraph*, "UN Condemns Israel's deadly attack on Gaza," 03/02/08, [accessed 5/2/09] http://www.telegraph.co.uk/news/worldnews/1580480/UN-condemns-Israels-deadly-attack-on-Gaza.html

9. "Quartet Statement, Sharm el-Sheikh, Egypt," 11/9/2008, [accessed 03/21/2009] http://www.un.org/News/dh/infocus/middle_east/quartet-9nov2008.htm

10. MSNBC.com: "Jews in Europe targeted over Gaza" 1/6/2009

11. Global Policy, "The Road Map," [accessed 5/21/09] http://www.globalpolicy.org/component/content/article/189/38357.html

12. PBS, "Former Prime Minister Tony Blair Named Middle East Envoy," 06/27/07 [accessed 04/26/09] http://www.pbs.org/newshour/updates/europe/jan-june07/blair_06-27.html

13. CBS, "Arab Nations To Attend Peace Conference," 11/23/07, [accessed 05/11/09 http://cbs5.com/national/annapolis.peace.conference.2.594310.html

14. Wikipedia Encyclopedia, Annapolis Conference, [accessed 05/07/09] http://en.wikipedia.org/wiki/Annapolis_Conference

15. *Reuters*, "Palestinian statehood deal possible in 2008-Blair," 06, Dec 2007 20:31:03 GMT http://www.alertnet.org/thenews/newsdesk/L06429153.htm

16. Hana Levi Julian, Arutz Sheva News, "Thousands Demonstrate in Jerusalem Against Annapolis Summit, 11/05/07 [accessed 5/12/09] http://www.israelnationalnews.com/News/News.aspx/124145

17. *Al Jazeera*, "Egypt to Attend Annapolis," [accessed 5/30/09] http://english. aljazeera.net/news/middleeast/2007/11/2008525124912176122.html

18. *Free Republic*, "School Books omit Israel – Palestinian Texts Studies," [accessed 4/12/09] http://www.freerepublic.com/focus/f-news/578102/posts

19. David Bedein, Israel Behind The News.com, "Abba Eban: the June 1967 map represented Israel's "Auschwitz" borders," 11/17/02, [accessed 6/04/09] http://www.mefacts.com/outgoing.asp?x_id=10191

20. Rory McCarthy & Tania Branigan, "Blair lands in Middle East," *Guardian/ UK*, July 23, 2007 article, http://www.guardian.co.uk/world/2007/jul/23/ israel.foreignpolicy/print accessed: March 23, 2009

21. "Blair Appointed Middle East Envoy," *BBC News* June 27, 2007 article http://news.bbc.co.uk/2/hi/uk_news/politics/6244358.stm accessed: March 23, 2009

22. *Israel Today*, "Israelis and Palestinians reach secret peace deal, says Blair," 12/10/08, [accessed 04/21/09, http://www.israeltoday.co.il/default. aspx?tabid=178&nid=17731

23. Aluf Benn & Barak Ravid, *Haaretz News*, "J'lem: Blair will seek to advance Israel-PA negotiations," 07/23/07, [accessed 05/23/09] http://www. haaretz.com/hasen/spages/884903.html

24. *USA Today*, "Blair arrives in Israel for first trip as Mideast envoy," 07/23/07, [accessed 05/22/09] http://www.usatoday.com/news/world/2007-07-23- blair-mideast_n.htm

25. *Israel Today*, "Israelis and Palestinians reach secret peace deal, says Blair," 12/10/08, [accessed 04/21/09, http://www.israeltoday.co.il/default. aspx?tabid=178&nid=17731

26. Bloomberg.com: "Libor-OIS Spread Chart," http://www.bloomberg.com/ apps/cbuilder?ticker1=.LOIS3%3AIND accessed: 03/23/09

27. Ibid

28. Ibid

29. Sam Jones, FT.Com/alphaville, "What price risk?" 09/25/08, http://ftalphaville.ft.com/blog/2008/09/25/16327/what-price-risk/

30. Bloomberg.com: "Libor-OIS Spread Chart," http://www.bloomberg.com/apps/cbuilder?ticker1=.LOIS3%3AIND accessed: 03/23/09

31. Sam Jones, FT.Com/alphaville, "What price risk?" 09/25/08, http://ftalphaville.ft.com/blog/2008/09/25/16327/what-price-risk/

32. Edward Harrison, "Libor-OIS Spread at an all time high," September 25, 2008 http://www.rgemonitor.com/financemarkets-monitor/253743/libor-ois_spread_at_an_all-time_high, [Accessed: 03/23/09]

33. Dan Weil, "Greenspan: Spread Shows Banks in Fear," Newsmax.com, February 26, 2009, http://moneynews.newsmax.com/printTemplate.html, [accessed: 03/23/09]

34. Jennifer Yousfi, "Credit Crisis Update: Foreign Stocks Dive Monday on Trio of European Bank Bailouts," "Investment News: Money Morning", http://www.moneymorning.com/2008/09/29/fortis/ [accessed: 03/23/09]

35. Gavin Finch, "Libor Rises Most on Record After U.S. Congress Rejects Bailout", September 30, 2008, Bloomberg.com, http://www.bloomberg.com/apps/news?pid=20601087&sid=a2r99gEsqU3k&refer=home [accessed 03/23/09]

36. Gabrielle Coppola & Liz Capo McCormick, "Libor's Creep Shows Credit Markets at Risk of Seizure", Bloomberg.com, March 11,2009, http://www.bloomberg.com/apps/news?pid=20670001&refer=home&sid=a0JxdKUPIyk4 accessed: March 23, 2009

37. "Behavior of Libor in the Current Financial Crisis," Federal Reserve Bank San Francisco Economic Letter- Number 2009-04 [January 23, 2009]

38. Sam Jones, FT.Com/alphaville, "What price risk?" 09/25/08, http://ftalphaville.ft.com/blog/2008/09/25/16327/what-price-risk/

39. Wikipedia Encyclopedia "Subprime Crisis http://en.wikipedia.org/wiki/Subprime_mortgage_crisis

40. Ibid

41. Council on Foreign Relations, "Timeline: Global Economy in Crisis," [accessed 02/24/09] http://www.cfr.org/publication/18709/

42. *Guardian.com*, "Banking crisis timeline," [accessed 3/13/09] www.guardian.co.uk/business/2008/oct/08/creditcrunch.marketturmoil

43. Ibid

44. Ibid

45. Ibid

46. Ibid

47. *New York Post mgray@nypost.com* http://www.nypost.com/seven/09212008/business/almost_armageddon_130110.htm

48. Ibid

49. Ibid

50. CNNMoney.com, "Greenspan: Economy in once in a lifetime crisis," [accessed 05/14/09] http://money.cnn.com/2008/09/14/news/economy/greenspan/

CHAPTER FOURTEEN

1. Wikipedia Encyclopedia, "Jerusalem" [accessed 05/02/09] http://en.wikipedia.org/wiki/Status_of_Jerusalem

2. Ibid

3. Teddy Kollek & Moshe Pearlman 1968 "Jerusalem" [accessed 05/04/09] http://www.zianet.com/maxey/proph12.htm

4. *New York Times,* May 21, 2000 "Jerusalem"

5. Wikipedia Encyclopedia, "Jerusalem" [accessed 05/02/09] http://en.wikipedia.org/wiki/Status_of_Jerusalem

6. Ibid

7. Ibid

8. Ibid

9. Ibid

10. Brian Whitaker, "Special Report: Israel and the Middle East," *Guardian Newspaper*--UK. http://www.guardian.co.uk/Archive/Article/0,4273,4053917,00.html

11. Wikipedia Encyclopedia "Temple Mount" [accessed 05/22/09] http://en.wikipedia.org/wiki/Temple_Mount

12. *Haaretz News*, "A provocation in religious clothing," 05/15/07, [accessed 05/03/09] http://www.haaretz.com/hasen/spages/859573.html

13. PalestineFacts.org, "Holy Sites Desecrated," [accessed 04/11/09] http://www.palestinefacts.org/pf_1948to1967_holysites.php

14. AboutBibleProphecy.org, "Zechariah," [accessed 05/04/09] http://www.aboutbibleprophecy.com/p72.htm

15. *Holy Bible*, King James Version, Book of Zechariah; Chapter 1

16. Ibid

17. *Holy Bible*, King James Version, Book of Zechariah; Chapter 12

18. Jerusalem Post Dec 16, 2008 "Rice cites Middle East peace moves at UN"

CHAPTER SIXTEEN

1. Tony Karon, "Despite Jewish Concerns, Obama Keeps Up Pressure on Israel," *Time*, July 14, 2009, [accessed 07/17/09] www.time.com/time/printout/0,8816,1910376,00.html

APPENDIX A

1. Wikipedia Encyclopedia, "Jewish History," [accessed 5/14/09] http://en.wikipedia.org/wiki/Jewish_history

2. Wikipedia Encyclopedia, "Abraham," [accessed 5/14/09] http://en.wikipedia.org/wiki/Abraham

3. *Holy Bible*, King James Version, Book of Genesis; Chapter 12

4. *Holy Bible*, King James Version, Book of Ezekiel; Chapter 47

5. Ibid

6. *Holy Bible*, King James Version, Book of Genesis; Chapter 12

7. *Holy Bible*, King James Version, Book of Genesis; Chapter 13

8. *Holy Bible*, King James Version, Book of Genesis; Chapter 26

9. *Holy Bible*, King James Version, Book of Genesis; Chapter 28

10. *Holy Bible*, King James Version, Book of Genesis; Chapter 35

11. Wikipedia Encyclopedia, Timeline of Jewish History," [accessed 5/11/09] http://en.wikipedia.org/wiki/Timeline_of_Jewish_history

12. Ibid

13. Ibid

14. Ibid

15. Wars of Israel, [accessed 02/12/09] http://www.warsofisrael. com/8victories.html#hazor

APPENDIX B

1. "Jewish Feasts and Holy Days," Millennium – Ark, [accessed 8/9/09] http://standeyo.com/News_Files/Inspire/Jewish_calender.html

2. *Holy Bible*, King James Version, Book of Ezekiel; Chapter 4

3. Ibid

4. *Holy Bible*, King James Version, Book of Leviticus; Chapter 26

5. Wikipedia Encyclopedia, "Babylonian captivity" [accessed 05/02/09] http://en.wikipedia.org/wiki/Babylonian_Captivity

6. Encyclopedia Britannica online, "Babylonian Exile," [accessed 8/9/09] http://www.britannica.com/EBchecked/topic/47693/Babylnian-Exile

7. John Pratt, "When Was Judah's 70-Year Babylonian Captivity?" The Ensign 28, 10/1998, http://www.johnpratt.com/items/docs/captivity.html

INDEX

CPSIA information can be obtained at www.ICGtesting.com
Printed in the USA
LVOW100704270113

317219LV00001BE/1/P